THE NEW BOWLING TRIVIA BOOK

BY DON WILLIAMS

EVERGREEN PUBLISHING GROUP, INC.
SOUTHFIELD, MICHIGAN

© **2003 by Don Williams**

ISBN: 0-923568-52-2

Cover Design and Chapter Illustrations by Bruce Worden

For Further Information, Please Contact:

Evergreen Publishing Group Inc.

28819 Franklin Road, Suite 710

Southfield, Michigan 48034

248-359-9990

www.bowlingtrivia.com

Library of Congress Cataloging-in-Publication Data

Williams, Donald (Donald Charles)
  The new bowling trivia book / by Don Williams.
    p. cm.
  ISBN 0-923568-52-2
    1. Bowling--Miscellanea.   I. Title. II. Title: Bowling
trivia book.
  GV904.W55 2003
  794.6--dc21

2003011287

Manufactured in the United States of America

To My Family
As always, you help make everything possible.

Contents

Foreword

Bowling. Whether or not you have ever bowled competitively, it is an activity that entertains, enthralls, and excites more than 100 million people worldwide. Very young children can play with bumpers and knock down pins with every throw without having any gutter balls. Senior citizens can compete and socialize regularly in leagues. High school competitors can represent their school and possibly even earn a varsity letter. Pro Bowlers can compete at the highest levels and dazzle everyone with their skill and determination. Physically challenged bowlers are able to enjoy the game and continually set records of their own. Bowling is truly the sport of a lifetime.

Bowling. Many new participants have enjoyed Glow Bowling, Rock 'n Bowl, Cosmic Bowling, or any of the aptly named modern variations. The music, lights, and special effects all lead to crowd excitement and a palpable energy. This is a sport with a rich and storied history. While not always getting the respect it deserves, bowling is used by dozens of companies to market hundreds of products. Bowling continues to evolve and react to current trends.

Bowling needs to trumpet its successes and revere its history. A continuation of progress and innovation should not forget the colorful past, while eyeing a potentially rich future.

Bowling. It's a perfect family activity, company outing, or first date. If it has been a few years, you owe it to yourself to see the amazing technologies and special effects. If you have not done so, tune in and watch the professionals, both men and women, compete for pride and prize money. Their achievements are truly amazing. Visit the Bowling Hall of Fame in St. Louis with friends or family. It is an experience that anyone would enjoy.

This book was written to give you some history, some background, some accomplishments, and some fun. After reading, standard procedure is to go bowling!

The First Frame:

A Colorful History

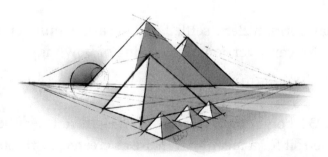

The earliest known objects used for a game similar to bowling date from 5200 B.C. Where were these objects found?

IN THE TOMB OF AN EGYPTIAN BOY BY SCIENTIST SIR FLINDERS PETRIE DURING THE 1930s.

An ancient Polynesian game in which the players rolled round stones at pins was called Ula Maika. This game has a unique similarity to modern bowling. What is this similarity?

THE DISTANCE BETWEEN THE BALL AND PINS USED IN ULA MAIKA WAS 60 FEET. THIS IS BASICALLY THE SAME AS TODAY'S SPECIFICATIONS.

When bowling at pins was popular in Germany, the participants did not consider the activity a sport. In what ceremony was bowling included?

MANY HISTORIANS BELIEVE BOWLING AT PINS WAS AN ACTIVITY THAT WAS INCLUDED IN RELIGIOUS RITES.

What German cleric settled on nine as the number of pins for early versions of Kegeling or bowling?

MARTIN LUTHER.

In 1932, bowling proprietors from eight states gathered in Detroit for a meeting. What was created by these bowling establishment owners that continues to this day?

THE BOWLING PROPRIETORS' ASSOCIATION OF AMERICA.

At this first meeting an official publication of the new organization was also named. Do you know the name of this publication?

THE BOWLERS' JOURNAL.

There is a section of land known as Bowling Green in Manhattan. How did the name of this area originate?

LAWN BOWLING WAS PLAYED BY BRITISH SETTLERS IN THIS AREA.

Remember the story of Rip Van Winkle who fell asleep for a very long time? What were the circumstances that led to Rip Van Winkle going into a long sleep?

HE DRANK FROM A KEG BELONGING TO A BAND OF LITTLE MEN WHO WERE PLAYING NINEPINS.

What royal decree did King Henry VIII issue in 1541?

ALL FORMS OF BOWLING WERE OUTLAWED IN ENGLAND.

When Henry VIII outlawed bowling, he gave three reasons for his actions. What were they?

HE BELIEVED THAT BOWLING HAD BECOME A VICIOUS FORM OF GAMBLING; HIS SOLDIERS WERE SPENDING TOO MUCH TIME BOWLING; AND HE BELIEVED BOWLING WAS ONLY A PRIVILEGE OF THE WEALTHY.

What occurred in the early 1840s that began a meteoric rise in the popularity of bowling?

INDOOR LANES OR ALLEYS APPEARED, THEREBY NEGATING WEATHER AS A FACTOR.

What was the name of the first organization in the United States that attempted to regulate tenpin bowling?

> THE NATIONAL BOWLING ASSOCIATION, WHICH WAS FORMED IN 1875.

In 1890, which short-lived organization followed the National Bowling Association?

> THE AMERICAN BOWLING LEAGUE.

In what year was the Professional Bowlers Association organized?

> 1958.

Who was the inventor of the first automatic pinsetter to meet sanctioned approval?

> FRED SCHMIDT. THE FIRST PROTOTYPE WAS BUILT IN HIS GARAGE.

This automatic pinsetter was first displayed at a tournament in Buffalo, New York. In what year was this?

> 1946.

The automatic pinsetter was not officially approved until 1952, when 12 machines were installed in a Midwestern city. Name the city that first received these machines.

> MT. CLEMENS, MICHIGAN.

What was the name of the bowling center in which these machines were installed?

THE BOWL O DROME.

In 1916, 40 women from 11 cities met to form a new organization. After several name changes, what present day organization was formed?

THE WOMEN'S INTERNATIONAL BOWLING CONGRESS.

In what city was this historical meeting held?

ST. LOUIS.

The merger of three different organizations formed the Young American Bowling Alliance. Can you name them?

YABA IS THE RESULT OF COMBINING THE AMERICAN JUNIOR BOWLING CONGRESS, THE ABC/WIBC COLLEGIATE DIVISION, AND THE YOUTH BOWLING ASSOCIATION.

USA Bowling is an organization that selects United States representatives for international competition. This organization was originally founded in 1989 under a different name. What was the original name?

THE UNITED STATES TENPIN BOWLING FEDERATION.

In what year did the Olympic games offer bowling competition?

IN 1936 IN BERLIN, GERMANY.

What American bowler won all bowling events during the 1936 Olympic competition?

HANK MARINO.

In 1942, a bowling group was organized to provide recreational equipment for servicemen and also to raise funds for veterans' programs. What was the name of this dedicated group?

THE BOWLERS VICTORY LEGION.

Sovereign Strikes

1. While King Henry VII was a resident of Whitehall Palace in the 1500s, he made several additions to this residence. What did he specifically create space for?

2. King Henry's daughter, Elizabeth I, continued to recognize bowling as a status symbol among the elite. What game did the nobility of the times play regularly at their estates?

1. He made space to accommodate indoor bowling.

2. Skittles. Many had specific skittle areas at their estates.

Women bowlers participated in programs to raise money for the armed services during World War II. One of these projects raised money to fund a Douglas Attack Bomber. Because of their efforts, what was this airplane named?

MISS WIBC, AFTER THE WOMEN'S INTERNATIONAL BOWLING CONGRESS.

In what year was the American Bowling Congress formed?

1895.

In what year did the American Bowling Congress organize the first U.S. national bowling tournament?

1901.

The Federation Internationale des Quilleurs is the world governing body of bowling. Known as the FIQ, it was originally founded in 1952. How many nations were part of the FIQ when it was founded?

NINE NATIONS. THE UNITED STATES DID NOT BECOME A MEMBER UNTIL 1961.

What company was founded in 1845 that eventually would evolve into a name synonymous with bowling?

JOHN MOSES BRUNSWICK FOUNDED THE COMPANY THAT WOULD BECOME THE BRUNSWICK CORPORATION.

In what year did Brunswick expand into bowling?

> IN 1890, THE BRUNSWICK CORPORATION BEGAN OFFERING WOODEN PINS AND BOWLING BALLS.

Bowling proprietor Bill Williams was elected the nineteenth President of the Bowling Proprietors' Association of America in 1962. This ambassador of bowling was also given two other BPAA awards. Can you name them?

> MR. WILLIAMS RECEIVED THE PRESIDENT'S MEDAL IN 1979 AND THE VICTOR LERNER MEMORIAL MEDAL FOR A LIFETIME OF SELFLESS SERVICE TO BOWLING IN 1981.

In the mid 1930s, the Bowling Proprietors' Association of America was struggling for funds. In addition to the annual dues, the association asked for an additional one dollar per lane to be donated by the member proprietor. What was this additional dollar fee known as?

> IT WAS CONSIDERED A "CLUB MEMBERSHIP." A PER LANE ASSESSMENT CONTINUES IN THE PRESENT DAY DUES STRUCTURE.

How many charter members were there when the Professional Bowlers Association was founded in 1958?

> THIRTY-THREE.

How many members does the new look PBA have now?

> OVER 4000 MEMBERS.

In 1901, the first ABC tournament was held in Chicago. What company was the sole supplier of lanes for this prestigious event?

THE BRUNSWICK CORPORATION.

In January of 1841, an edition of the *Hartford Daily Courant* ran a story about a Grogshop or tavern. With this story came a specific "first." What was it?

THIS GROGSHOP INCLUDED A TENPIN ALLEY IN FULL OPERATION, WHICH IS POSSIBLY THE VERY FIRST PUBLISHED REFERENCE TO THE GAME OF TENPINS.

During the early 1300s in Germany, approval was given to bowling games. This opened the sport to many people, allowing it to eventually become part of village festivals. Who granted this endorsement?

THE CATHOLIC CHURCH.

Many credit three contributing factors — all beginning with the letter "A" — for upgrading and expanding the image of bowling. The first is automation. What are the other two?

ARCHITECTURE AND AIR CONDITIONING.

During the 1941-42 season, a national war bond tournament was held. What was the name of this tournament that was displayed on posters in many bowling centers?

KEEP 'EM ROLLIN.' IT WAS A SLOGAN TO SUPPORT OUR MILITARY DURING WORLD WAR II.

During the Prohibition years, a report was issued by *The Journal of the American Medical Association* that referenced bowling. Why did physicians recommend bowling?

"BECAUSE IT EXERCISES UNUSED MUSCLES OF THE BODY AND CAN BE PLAYED YEAR ROUND."

In the early days of bowling, what score was considered a perfect game?

200.

In the early days of American Bowling Congress Tournaments, what prizes were used to reward winners?

THEIR PRIZE WINNINGS WERE PAID IN GOLD COINS.

John McGraw and Wilbert Robinson were baseball people who also became bowling proprietors. What tenpin-related bowling game did these gentlemen create?

THEY CREATED THE GAME OF DUCKPINS BY TURNING DOWN SOME OF THEIR PINS AND REDUCING THE SIZE OF THE BOWLING BALLS.

This game grew so popular that a National Duckpin Bowling Congress was organized. In what year was this association started?

1927.

The original meeting to establish the American Bowling Congress was held in a building known as Beethoven Hall. Prior to this historic meeting, what other bowling business had been conducted in Beethoven Hall?

THIS NEW YORK CITY BUILDING WAS THE HEADQUARTERS OF THE UNITED BOWLING CLUBS.

Every bowler who donated to the Bowlers Victory Legion received a gift of an embroidered emblem. What two words adorned this symbolic patch?

ALONG WITH THE BVL LOGO WERE THE WORDS "I GAVE."

During World War II, posters asking bowlers to "Bowl over the Axis" encouraged the purchase of war bonds. What were some of the items that could be funded with war bond purchases?

WAR BONDS TOTALING $500,000 ALLOWED THE DONOR TO NAME A HEAVY BOMBER; $150,000 IN BONDS WOULD NAME A PURSUIT SHIP; AND $75,000 IN BONDS WOULD SPONSOR A TANK.

Because of the critical labor shortages during World War II, many bowling centers were forced to close their doors. A shortage of what type of employee was critical to a bowling center's operation?

BEFORE THE INVENTION OF AUTOMATIC EQUIPMENT, PIN BOYS WERE A NECESSITY TO STAY IN BUSINESS.

The American Bowling Congress, the Women's International Bowling Congress, and the American Junior Bowling Congress all barred people of color from participating in the tournaments they sponsored in the 1940s. After World War II, what outside pressure began to change these policies?

THE UNITED AUTOWORKERS' UNION IN 1947, AND THE INTERNATIONAL LADIES' GARMENT UNION IN 1948, THREATENED TO WITHDRAW SPONSORSHIP OF TOURNAMENTS AND LEAGUES THAT EXCLUDED MINORITIES.

In what year did the American Bowling Congress agree to integrate competition?

1950.

The Women's International Bowling Congress raised funds to purchase several warplanes during World War II. In 1944, what was the name of the campaign by the WIBC that led to the purchase of an ambulance plane?

THE WINGS OF MERCY.

In October of 1943, the National Bowling Congress was formed in Chicago. It was made up of bowling proprietors, officials of the American Bowling Congress, and representatives of bowling manufacturers. What crisis brought this organization together?

THE UNITED STATES GOVERNMENT PROPOSED INSTITUTING A TAX ON BOWLING.

In 1941, the American Bowling Congress took a patriotic step that affected thousands of bowlers. What did the ABC do?

THE ABC PROVIDED, FREE OF CHARGE, SANCTIONING AND CERTIFICATION TO ALL LEAGUES, BOWLERS, AND ESTABLISHMENTS OF THE ARMED FORCES.

In what year were the headquarters of the American Bowling Congress located in Milwaukee, Wisconsin built?

1952. AN EXPANSION WAS ADDED IN 1961.

What United States President was the catalyst behind the installation of bowling lanes in the White House?

HARRY TRUMAN.

President Truman was photographed often while bowling. A widely published photo of the President bowling left-handed in the White House shows some unusual aspects. What were they?

THE PRESIDENT IS WEARING A THREE-PIECE SUIT AND BLACK STREET SHOES WHILE BOWLING.

Three businessmen purchased the Professional Bowlers Association in March of 2000. What does this trio of businessmen have in common?

ALL ARE FORMER MICROSOFT EXECUTIVES.

In what year was the National Negro Bowling
Association formed?

> 1939. THIS ORGANIZATION LATER BECAME THE NATIONAL
> BOWLING ASSOCIATION, INC.

In 1978, J. Elmer Reed was inducted into the American
Bowling Congress Hall of Fame. Why was this a
groundbreaking event?

> MR. REED WAS THE FIRST BLACK INDUCTED INTO THE ABC
> HALL OF FAME. HE WAS A PIONEER OF THE NATIONAL
> NEGRO BOWLING ASSOCIATION.

The Second Frame:

It's Showtime!

In 1960, NBC produced a national bowling television show. Name the show and its host.

"JACKPOT BOWLING;" THE POPULAR SHOW WAS HOSTED BY COMEDIAN MILTON BERLE.

Philips once released a hi-fi record titled "Bowl 'Em Over." A lot of bonus points if you can name the group featured on this record.

THE SERENDIPITY SINGERS.

In the movie *The Flintstones*, what was the name of the bowling center that Fred and Barney frequented?

THE BEDROCK BOWL O RAMA.

Fred Flintstone and Barney Rubble were on the same bowling team. What was the name of their team?

THE WATER BUFFALOS.

A rather obscure movie was released with the title *Mystery Men*. One of the characters is called "the bowler." Any idea which actress played this character?

JANEANE GAROFALO.

In the movie she uses a unique bowling ball as a weapon. What was unique about it?

THE BALL IS CLEAR WITH THE SKULL OF HER LATE FATHER IN IT.

In 1975, there was a popular television show known as the "Superstars Competition." Athletes from many different sports competed for prize money. What "superstar" contestant credited his victory in bowling as the key to winning the overall competition?

O.J. Simpson.

Bowling even shows up on the hit show "Law & Order SVU." During an episode airing in February of 2003, what bowling center is featured?

Rock & Roll Bowl.

An often forgotten television show that featured bowling aired during the '70s. What was the name of the show that began in 1971?

"Celebrity Bowling."

What was the format of "Celebrity Bowling?"

Four celebrities competed in teams of two. One celeb from each of the two teams threw their first ball. Of the two bowlers, the one who knocked down more pins on the first ball had their partner try to make the easier of the two spares. Ten frames were bowled with prizes awarded to members of the studio audience based on their performance.

What score would win a member of the studio audience a new car?

210.

How many times did a member of the studio audience win a new car?

THIS WAS ONLY ACCOMPLISHED ONCE. TWO ACTORS FROM THE TV SHOW "MOD SQUAD," TIGE ANDREWS AND MICHAEL COLE, WERE HEROES TO THE AUDIENCE MEMBER WHO WON THE CAR.

Besides these two actors, can you name at least six other celebrities that appeared on the show?

STEVE ALLEN, ED AMES, RICHARD DAWSON, ROY ROGERS, WILLIAM SHATNER, SID CAESAR, SAMMY DAVIS JR., MICHAEL DOUGLAS, PHYLLIS DILLER, AND ADAM WEST WOULD ALL QUALIFY.

"Celebrity Bowling" ceased production after the 1977-78 season. It did have a brief rebirth in 1987. What was the new title in 1987?

"THE NEW CELEBRITY BOWLING." IT WAS HOSTED BY JED ALLAN, WHO ALSO HOSTED THE ORIGINAL SERIES.

In April of 1950, a "bowling theme song" was introduced at the 47th American Bowling Congress Championships. What was the name of this bowling song?

"ROLL ON," WHICH WAS WRITTEN BY ERV CRAIG.

Name the movie whose story line featured the rags-to-riches tale of a professional bowler.

THIS 1979 RELEASE WAS TITLED *DREAMER*.

Name the actor who portrayed the professional bowler in the movie *Dreamer*.

TIM MATHESON.

A movie distributed by Columbia Pictures titled *Ten Pin Magic* was a truly unique bowling movie at the time. Why?

TEN PIN MAGIC FEATURED AUTOMATIC PINSETTERS.

Can you name at least three television sitcoms that featured episodes that took place in a bowling center?

"THE HONEYMOONERS," "ALL IN THE FAMILY," "ROSEANNE," "LAVERNE AND SHIRLEY," "MARRIED WITH CHILDREN," AND "THE ANDY GRIFFITH SHOW" WOULD ALL QUALIFY.

What was the name of the popular television bowling show that featured local viewers as contestants competing for cash prizes?

"BOWLING FOR DOLLARS."

The members of this traveling group were involved in a transcontinental bowling league that competed in cities the group visited. What famous entertainment troupe in the 1940s participated in this unique cross-country league?

THE ICE FOLLIES.

Radio station WXYZ in Detroit, Michigan featured a bowling show called "The 10 Pin Talker." Who was the host of this popular show?

> FRED WOLF. THIS MEMBER OF THE AMERICAN BOWLING CONGRESS HALL OF FAME WAS THE FIRST TO PUT BOWLING TOURNAMENTS ON THE AIRWAYS LOCALLY IN THE DETROIT AREA.

For twelve years beginning in 1956, Mr. Wolf was the voice of "Championship Bowling." However, in 1961, Mr. Wolf was involved in an important event. What was this groundbreaking first?

> FRED WOLF DID THE COMMENTARY FOR THE FIRST PBA TELEVISED TOURNAMENT IN NEW JERSEY. THIS TOURNAMENT WAS USED TO SELL THE PBA TO ABC.

In the famous comic strip "Peanuts," what nickname did Snoopy use while bowling?

> JOE SANDBAGGER. THIS BOWLING RELATED STRIP APPEARED IN 1982.

To the dismay of his bowling buddies, what was Joe Sandbagger's bowling average?

> ONE.

Who was the first professional bowler to appear on the "Ed Sullivan Show?"

> WAYNE ZAHN.

Which Brunswick Corporation sponsored TV show had a three-year run on American television?

"Bowling Shootout."

On the sitcom "Married with Children," an episode that first aired in March of 1990 had Al Bundy planning a special evening for his wife Peg's birthday. Of course they were going to go bowling, but where?

Al's plans were for a big evening at the Bowlarama.

While bowling with Peggy that night, Al's plan was to break his arch rival's high game record. While Al actually broke the long-standing record, what ruined his night?

Moments after Al broke his rival's record, Peggy bowled a perfect game.

In another classic "Married with Children" episode, Al pretends to be scared by shoes because of a robbery at his shoe store. What must Al sacrifice to win the bowling championship?

Because Al was not allowed to bowl barefoot, he had to choose between an insurance settlement and winning the championship.

On the very popular "The Andy Griffith Show," which Mayberry resident bowled a 300 game?

Howard Sprague, while he was a member of the Mayberry Bowling Team.

Who were the other members of the Mayberry team?

HOWARD BOWLED WITH ANDY TAYLOR AND GOOBER
PYLE.

Who was the sponsor of the Mayberry bowling team?

EMMETT CLARK'S FIX IT SHOP.

Andy Taylor also bowled in another league from time
to time. What was the name of this league?

THE PEACE OFFICERS LEAGUE.

Archie Bunker bowled during several episodes of "All
In The Family." During an episode that aired
December 16, 1972, what bowling team did Archie try
to join?

THE CANNONBALLERS.

Why did Archie not make the team?

HE WAS BLACKBALLED IN ORDER TO ALLOW ANOTHER
PLAYER TO TAKE HIS PLACE ON THE TEAM.

The actor Fred MacMurray delivered the following line
in a famous 1944 movie, "...I didn't want to go back to
the office, so I dropped by a bowling alley at Third and
Western and rolled a few lines..." Can you name the
movie?

DOUBLE INDEMNITY. YOU HAVE TO LOVE A MOVIE THAT
FEATURES BOWLING AND AN INSURANCE SALESMAN.

On "The Simpsons," Homer buys Marge a bowling ball
for her birthday. Why was Marge upset over this
seemingly nice gesture?

> HOMER HAD IT DRILLED TO FIT HIM AND HAD HIS NAME
> ENGRAVED ON IT.

Homer joins a secret organization called the
Stonecutters. When he goes bowling with the
Stonecutters what lane does he bowl on?

> LANE 13.

What is the name of the local bowling pro and
womanizer who gives Marge bowling lessons?

> JACQUES.

How much does Jacques charge for a bowling lesson?
For extra credit, how much does he charge Marge?

> HE CHARGES $40 FOR A BOWLING LESSON BUT ONLY $25
> FOR MARGE.

The first time Marge meets Jacques she mistakenly calls
him by the name on his bowling ball. What does she
call him?

> BRUNSWICK.

What is unique about Jacques in the town of
Springfield?

> HE IS THE ONLY BOWLER IN SPRINGFIELD TO HAVE
> GROUPIES.

BOWLING IN PRIMETIME

The Simpson family bowls at which bowling center?

    A. BEN'S BOWL-O-DROME

    B. BOB'S BOWLING LANES

    C. BARNEY'S BOWL-A-RAMA

    D. BILL'S BOWLING & TACKLE SHOP

Many bowling leagues have banquets at the end of the season. On "The Honeymooners," the Raccoon bowling team held a victory feast with three types of pizza. Which of the four choices below was not one of the available pizza choices for their bowling banquet?

    A. PIG'S KNUCKLES

    B. NEAPOLITAN KNOCKWURST

    C. SOHO SAUSAGE

    D. SAUERKRAUT

Which of the following teams did the Raccoons beat for the championship?

    A. BUSHWICK

    B. FLUSHING

    C. SECAUCUS

    D. BAYONNE

1. The answer is "C," Barney's Bowl-A-Rama.
2. The answer is "C." Soho sausage was not a pizza option.
3. D. The answer is Bayonne. During the championship Ralph went on to win an MVP trophy.

To complete the bowling theme during an episode of "The Simpsons," what is behind Marge and Jacques during an outdoor scene?

THE MOON, COMPLETE WITH THREE HOLES LIKE A BOWLING BALL.

During an episode originally aired in February of 1992, what does Simpson baby Maggie do to Homer's bowling uniform?

SHE SPILLS MILK ALL OVER THE FRESHLY DRY-CLEANED UNIFORM.

The Simpson children beg their parents to take them to Itchy & Scratchy Land. Reading from the brochure, Bart says it isn't just for kids. They have a place called "Parents' Island." Besides dancing and fashionable shops, what else can parents do?

GO BOWLING.

Even though it appears that Homer only uses bowling for competition and relaxation, in reality he has a much deeper history with bowling. What is it?

HE ONCE TOOK A JOB WORKING AT THE LOCAL BOWLING ALLEY.

When Homer had to leave the bowling alley for another job, what did the crew at the bowling alley give him as a gift?

A SATIN JACKET WITH THE WORDS "SORRY YOU HAD TO SPLIT" STITCHED ON THE BACK.

During his employment at the bowling alley, Homer gives a famous quote. Do you know what it is?

"IF HORSERACING IS THE SPORT OF KINGS, THEN SURELY BOWLING IS A...VERY GOOD SPORT AS WELL."

Homer arrives at a collectible shop and notices the owner of the shop is wearing what?

A SECONDHAND BOWLING SHIRT FROM GOODWILL, WITH THE NAME HOMER STITCHED ON THE FRONT.

What is another connection the television cartoon show "The Simpsons" has with bowling?

DURING ONE EPISODE, THE ENTIRE SIMPSON FAMILY TRAVELED TO ST. LOUIS TO VISIT THE NATIONAL BOWLING HALL OF FAME.

What special souvenir did the Simpson family leave the Hall of Fame with?

THEY HAD A FAMILY PICTURE TAKEN IN FRONT OF THE BOWLING PIN CAR ON DISPLAY IN THE HALL OF FAME.

When Lisa Simpson won the state spelling bee, what did her brother Bart say about her trophy?

"FINALLY, THE SIMPSONS HAVE A TROPHY WITHOUT A BOWLING BALL."

On the television show "The Honeymooners," Ralph Cramden was a member of what bowling team?

THE RACCOON LODGE TEAM.

In what city did Ralph Cramden and Ed Norton bowl most often on the television show "The Honeymooners?"

Brooklyn, New York.

In an episode known as "Letter to the Boss," Ralph Cramden and Ed Norton are trying to decide how to remove a letter from a mailbox. During the conversation a policeman overhears their plotting. Where does this plotting occur?

In a bowling alley locker room.

You are a trivia whiz if you know the name of the bowling alley that appeared in some episodes of "The Honeymooners." Name the alley.

Melacrina's Bowling Alley.

In an episode known as "Oh My Aching Back," what fashion statement labels Ralph and Ed as bowlers?

They both wear their Raccoon bowling team jackets.

Sticking with clothing, what does Ed do to Ralph's bowling jacket during another episode?

He burns the jacket while trying to iron it.

But Ed does not always do the wrong thing. What did Ed do for Ralph when Ralph sprained his ankle at the bowling alley?

Ed carried Ralph home piggyback.

Getting back to Ralph and Ed trying to get a letter out of a mailbox, do you know where the mailbox was located?

IN FRONT OF THE BOWLING ALLEY.

Ralph wants to compete in the bowling championship. Alice has other ideas. What does his wife want him to do instead?

SHE WANTS HIM TO GO TO A FAMILY GET-TOGETHER AT HER MOTHER'S HOUSE TO SEE HER UNCLE LEO.

What bowling accessory did Alice give Ralph for Christmas?

A BOWLING BAG.

By the way, what was the name of the Raccoons' bowling team?

THE HURRICANES.

In the 1948 movie *Road House*, Ida Lupino and Cornel Wilde are a lounge singer and a manager at what bowling center?

JEFTYS. RICHARD WIDMARK AND CELESTE HOLM ALSO STAR.

In the early 1932 classic *Scarface*, Paul Muni guns down what famous actor while he happily bowls at the local lanes?

BORIS KARLOFF.

In a more recent classic movie, the bad guy played by Robert Mitchum follows the family of Gregory Peck to a bowling center one evening. Can you name this 1962 film?

CAPE FEAR.

This television female comedy duo often frequented bowling centers. One of the characters always had her initial embroidered on her bowling shirts. Who were these ladies?

LAVERNE AND SHIRLEY.

In 1934, during a magazine interview, Ginger Rogers listed bowling as one of her two favorite leisure activities. What was the other activity?

HORSEBACK RIDING.

NBC once televised a popular morning quiz show called "Say When." This show was seen by more than a million viewers. What bowling product was offered as a prize to the contestants on this show?

A WARDROBE OF DEXTER BOWLING SHOES.

The world-famous Vienna Boys Choir was present at a bowling related event in 1961. With what event were they involved?

THEY PERFORMED AT THE OPENING OF A NEW BOWLING CENTER IN AUSTRIA.

Can you name the professional bowler who appeared on the televised game show "To Tell The Truth?"

BILL BATTISTA.

In yet another movie that involves a scene in a bowling center, Timothy Hutton and Elizabeth McGovern go bowling. Can you name this 1980 movie?

ORDINARY PEOPLE.

When Ms. McGovern delivers the ball, how many pins does she knock down?

0, SHE GETS A GUTTER BALL.

The HBO Series "Real Sports" recently aired a segment on bowling. What was the specific subject matter?

THE SHOW CENTERED ON THE PROFESSIONAL BOWLERS ASSOCIATION.

If you ran across the name Bowling for Soup, what would you have discovered?

BOWLING FOR SOUP IS A BAND THAT HAS RELEASED SEVERAL CDs. THEIR "DRUNK ENOUGH TO DANCE" TITLE WAS RELEASED IN AUGUST OF 2002.

During a bowling-related episode of the cartoon "Rugrats," the twins Phil and Lil want to help their mom do what?

THE TWINS WANT TO HELP THEIR MOM BETTY BRING HOME A TROPHY FROM STRIKES R US.

In 1934, MGM Studios produced a bowling movie. What was the title of that movie?

STRIKES AND SPARES.

This movie starred Andy Varipapa, in which he bowled trick shot after trick shot. What famous Varipapa trick shot performed in this movie was known as the "tunnel shot?"

TO PICK UP A ONE PIN SPARE, HE BOWLED THROUGH THE LEGS OF SHOWGIRLS STANDING ON THE LANE.

In 1944, the motion picture *Since You Went Away* was produced starring Robert Walker and Jennifer Jones. What reason did the producer give for including bowling scenes in this movie?

IT WAS A STORY OF THE AMERICAN HOME FRONT DURING THE WAR AND THE PRODUCER THOUGHT THAT BOWLING WAS AN INTEGRAL PART OF EVERYDAY LIFE DURING THIS TIME.

In a "Walker Texas Ranger" episode that guest starred Ernest Borgnine as a wrestling promoter, several scenes were shot in a bowling center. Can you name this featured bowling center?

BRONCO BOWL.

The well-known cartoon series "Scooby Doo" had a bowling-themed episode. Any guesses on the episode title?

"SCOOBY DOO AND THE BOWLING BOOGEYMAN."

Big Screen

Okay, golf has *Caddyshack*, and baseball has *Major League*. Like it or not, bowling has the movie *Kingpin*. Let's test your knowledge.

1. Match the character with the actor that played him.

ERNIE MCCRACKEN   WOODY HARRELSON

ISHMAEL   BILL MURRAY

ROY MUNSON   RANDY QUAID

2. What type of bowling ball did Ernie McCracken use during the finals?

3. Who was victorious in the final match between Roy Munson and Ernie McCracken? What was the final score?

4. What souvenir did Ernie McCracken throw to the crowd after the victory?

5. Please fill in the blank. "_____did for bowling what Muhammad Ali did for boxing."

6. What was the name of the tournament?

7. One of the following people did not appear as himself in the movie. Can you pick out the correct choice?

A. PBA BOWLER PARKER BOHN

B. ESPN ANNOUNCER CHRIS BERMAN

C. PBA BOWLER MARK ROTH

D. ESPN ANNOUNCER DAN PATRICK

8. Where is the championship held?

10. A. He did not appear in a bowling shirt with the name Billy.

QUAID, ANGEL - *KINGPIN*

9. FOX, DOUGLAS, TRAVIS - *GREEDY*; BRIDGES, GOODMAN, MOORE - *THE BIG LEBOWSKI*; HARRELSON,

Bowling

9. Can you match the stars with the bowling movie that they appeared in?

Michael J. Fox,
Kirk Douglas,
Nancy Travis

The Big Lebowski,
which was released in 1998

Jeff Bridges,
John Goodman,
Julianne Moore

Kingpin,
which was released in 1996

Woody Harrelson,
Randy Quaid,
Vanessa Angel

Greedy,
which was released in 1994

10. In *The Big Lebowski,* one member of the Dude's bowling circle was Donny. Donny always wore different bowling shirts. Which of the following names did not appear on the front of one of his bowling shirts?

    A. BILLY ON A BLACK SHIRT.

    B. AUSTIN ON A YELLOW SHIRT.

    C. JOEY ON A BLUE SHIRT.

    D. RAY ON A WHITE SHIRT.

8. THE NATIONAL BOWLING STADIUM IN RENO.

7. D. DAN PATRICK DID NOT APPEAR IN THE MOVIE.

6. BRUNSWICK RENO OPEN.

5. ERNIE MCCRACKEN

4. MUNSON'S RUBBER HAND.

3. MCCRACKEN DEFEATED MUNSON 226 TO 225.

2. IT WAS A CLEAR BALL WITH A ROSE INSIDE.

1. ERNIE MCCRACKEN - BILL MURRAY; ISHMAEL - RANDY QUAID; ROY MUNSON - WOODY HARRELSON

Even the HBO series "The Sopranos" does not escape a bowling connection. Even though it is somewhat morbid, what happened?

> CHRISTOPHER AND TONY PUT THE SEVERED HEAD OF JOEY INTO A BOWLING BAG FOR DISPOSAL.

For extra credit, any idea on how they disposed of the bowling bag containing the head?

> THEY HOT WIRED A BACKHOE, DUG A HOLE, AND BURIED THE BOWLING BAG.

Although fictional, the only bowling proprietor character to ever appear in a primetime series was Ed Stevens, who appears on the television series "Ed." What city is that bowling center located in?

> STUCKEYVILLE, WHICH HAPPENS TO BE ED'S HOME TOWN.

Because the bowling business was not booming for Ed, what unusual step did he take?

> HE SETS UP A LAW PRACTICE IN THE BOWLING ALLEY.

When working in the courtrooms, Ed was given an undesirable nickname. Do you know what it was?

> "THE BOWLING ALLEY LAWYER."

Milton Berle was the host of "Jackpot Bowling" in 1960-61. However, this show originally began in 1959. What was the original name of the popular show?

> "PHILLIES JACKPOT BOWLING."

Can you name any of the three hosts of "Phillies Jackpot Bowling" in 1959?

MEL ALLEN, LEO DUROCHER, AND BUD PALMER.

When "Jackpot Bowling" starring Milton Berle was on the air, the show was shown live from a Hollywood bowling alley. Between the matches, the show featured a celebrity of the week. How did the celebrity participate?

BETWEEN MATCHES THEY ROLLED A BALL FOR CHARITY.

In a 1955 documentary titled "Headpin Hints," professional bowlers Lee Jouglard and Sylvia Wene give instructions to young bowlers. Who was the narrator of this film?

FRED WOLF.

Near the end of "Headpin Hints," what did the two professionals do?

THEY DEMONSTRATED THE TECHNIQUE FOR PICKING UP DIFFICULT SPARES.

Another film short titled *Strikes and Spares* was released in 1934. Pete Smith was the narrator of this film but do you know the star?

ANDY VARIPAPA. IN THIS FILM SHORT ANDY DEMONSTRATES CORRECT GRIP, PROPER FORM AND FINALLY PERFORMS SEVERAL TRICK SHOTS.

Strikes and Spares was unique in another way. As a novelty film short, what honor did it receive?

IT WAS NOMINATED FOR AN OSCAR.

Later is his career, Mr. Varipapa starred in another film short titled *Bowling Tricks*. This film was also narrated by Mr. Smith. What year was this film released?

1948.

On the long running television show "Happy Days," Howard and Marion were members of a bowling team. What was the name of their team?

THE TENPINS.

Of course bowling history goes way back, including bowling film history. A bowling film titled *The Bowling Match* was a comedy. What is unusual about this film?

IT WAS A SILENT MOVIE SHOT IN BLACK AND WHITE THAT WAS RELEASED IN 1913. FOR THE RECORD, THE TWO STARS WERE MABEL NORMAND AND FORD STERLING.

In the movie *The Big Lebowski*, Jeff Bridges plays a character known as the "Dude." There is a picture hanging inside the Dude's home of an American President bowling. Can you identify this President?

RICHARD NIXON IS SHOWN BOWLING ON A POSTER OVER THE BAR.

Talk about a dedicated bowler. The Dude is shown lying on the rug in his place listening to a cassette tape. What was he listening to?

THE "A" SIDE OF THE CASSETTE FEATURING THE SOUNDS OF BOWLING FROM THE VENICE BEACH LEAGUE PLAYOFFS IN 1987.

The bowling alley hustler featured in the movie was named Jesus. What did Jesus wear on his left hand? How about his right hand?

THE CHARACTER JESUS WORE THREE HIGH SCORE AWARD RINGS ON HIS LEFT HAND AND A COBRA WRIST SUPPORT ON HIS RIGHT.

In the bowling center that is shown repeatedly in the movie, what is stated on the banner hanging over the center of the lanes?

STARS AND STRIKES FOREVER.

During the opening credits, the counter man of the bowling center is shown doing what?

DEODORIZING RENTAL SHOES.

There are two sponsors that appear frequently in the movie. Can you name them?

BRUNSWICK BOWLING AND MILLER BREWING PRODUCTS.

In the movie, what is the real name of the Dude?

JEFFREY LEBOWSKI.

The Comedy Central show "Let's Bowl" first aired in March of 1999. Do you remember the contestants from this inaugural show?

MARGIE VS. MIRA WITH MARGIE EMERGING VICTORIOUS.

When "Let's Bowl" was extended to a second season, what bowling center was used to film the second season action?

WELLS LANES IN ST. PAUL, MINNESOTA.

The Third Frame:

It's True

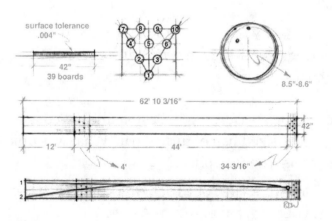

surface tolerance
.004"

42"
39 boards

8.5"-8.6"

62' 10 3/16"

42"

12'

44'

4'

34 3/16"

1
2

This is truly a question for this chapter. In what comic book did the two page story titled "Bowling: America's No. 1 Indoor Sport" appear?

IN MARCH OF 1942, THE NO. 10 ISSUE OF TRUE COMICS.

What branch of the U.S. Military issued a unit patch that featured a bowling ball knocking down pins?

U.S. ARMY 19TH BOMBARDMENT SQUADRON.

In the late 1800s, many saloon owners installed bowling alleys and billiard tables in their establishments for a particular reason. Any guesses?

BOTH WERE INSTALLED WITH THE INTENTION OF INCREASING ALCOHOL SALES.

Believe it or not, there is a bowling film titled *Sorority Babes in the Slimeball Bowl-O-Rama*. Any guesses on the plot?

FRATERNITY PLEDGES MUST GO TO THE LOCAL BOWLING CENTER AND STEAL A TROPHY. WHEN THE TROPHY BREAKS, CHAOS ENSUES.

Archaeologists working in Boston uncovered a grapefruit-sized ball of turned oak. What was unique about this wooden sphere?

THIS FIND TURNED OUT TO BE THE OLDEST KNOWN BOWLING BALL DISCOVERED IN NORTH AMERICA.

The archaeologists eventually dated this bowling ball. How old was it?

THEY DATED THE BALL TO THE 1660s.

The gonzo journalist Hunter S. Thompson is a page two columnist for ESPN. He recently wrote a satirical article about bowling. Can you imagine the title?

THE ARTICLE WAS ENTITLED "THE TRAGEDY OF NAKED BOWLING."

It could be argued that the silent-film star Harold Lloyd was the finest celebrity bowler ever. What would earn him that honor?

MR. LLOYD BOWLED AT LEAST ONE 300 GAME AND WAS ALSO A BOWLING PROPRIETOR.

According to a report from The Federation Internationale des Quilleurs, 80 countries have people who regularly bowl. How many participants come from this group of eighty countries?

ESTIMATES OF AS MANY AS 100 MILLION REGULAR BOWLERS.

According to a report of the top 30 participation activities in the United States, what is the number one activity based on participants aged 6 and older?

BASED ON 2002 NUMBERS, BOWLING IS THE NUMBER ONE ACTIVITY WITH OVER FIFTY THREE MILLION PARTICIPANTS. AS A COMPARISON, PARTICIPATION IN GOLF RANKS FOURTEENTH WITH ABOUT 28 MILLION.

According to a worldwide market research firm, what percentage of college students went bowling during the past year?

> 53% RESPONDED THAT THEY WENT BOWLING AT LEAST ONCE DURING THE PREVIOUS YEAR.

You can rent another unique bowling movie with a character known as Buzz Fizzelli, a bowling legend. Good luck looking for the title of this 1992 film. What was it?

> *SPARE ME.* IN IT A PROFESSIONAL BOWLER IS BANNED FROM COMPETING AFTER HITTING A COMPETITOR ON THE HEAD WITH A BOWLING BALL.

How much pressure impacts the lane when a 16-pound bowling ball meets the surface?

> APPROXIMATELY 1,800 POUNDS PER SQUARE INCH.

The National Sanitary Sales Company distributed this rather unique product during the 1950s with a bowling motif on the package. You will never guess this one.

> "SPARES" PROPHYLACTICS INCLUDED BOWLING BALL AND PIN ARTWORK ON THE PACKAGE.

If you were using the well-known Google Internet search engine on a typical spring day in 2003 and entered the word "bowling," how many hits would you receive?

> IN APRIL OF 2003 THERE WERE 4,800,000 HITS.

Bowling

1. What former baseball player and manager bowled a 515 series in his debut as a participant in an ABC tournament held in Chicago, Illinois?

2. Phil Rizzuto and Yogi Berra were partners in a New York bowling establishment. Can you name another baseball star that owned a center in Pennsylvania?

and 3. In 1955, what major league baseball team placed a bowling lane on the baseball playing field for a bowling exposition?

4. What bowler appeared as the star of that exposition?

5. What former baseball great, as the head of the President's Council on Physical Fitness, was known to demonstrate his left-handed bowling delivery?

5. STAN MUSIAL.
4. ANDY VARIPAPA.
3. CINCINNATI REDS.
2. NELLIE FOX, BASEBALL'S MVP IN 1959.
ANNOUNCER AT THE TIME.
1. LOU BOUDREAU, WHO WAS A CHICAGO CUBS BASEBALL

Baseball

For a bowling team who competed in 1966, the number "1950" had special meaning. What did this number represent?

> IT WAS THE COMBINED WEIGHT OF THE FIVE-MAN TEAM. THEIR INDIVIDUAL WEIGHTS WERE 300, 365, 473, 366, AND 446.

Around 1956, you could enter a bowling center and encounter Gutter Gus and Gutter Gussie who were both about 8 feet tall. Who were these giants?

> THEY WERE BOWLING THEMED FIGURES CREATED BY A CARTOONIST TO DECORATE BOWLING CENTERS.

If you purchased a Bowling Champ Barbie you would receive a Barbie doll dressed in an early era bowling outfit complete with shoes, bag, and ball. There is also one other accessory included. What is it?

> A BOWLING TROPHY.

If someone asked you about the "system of bowling" what would they be referring to?

> THERE ARE FOUR COMPONENTS THAT MAKE UP THE SCORING ENVIRONMENT OF BOWLING. THEY ARE THE BALL, PINS, LANE DRESSING, AND LANE SURFACE. THIS IS CONSIDERED THE SYSTEM OF BOWLING.

What is the minimum number of balls that can be thrown during a game of bowling?

> THE ANSWER IS 11. NINE STRIKES IN A ROW AND TWO BALLS IN THE TENTH FRAME.

When visiting the Detroit area you can visit the
Cadieux Café, which is a unique Belgian Restaurant.
While there you can Feather Bowl. Why is it called
Feather Bowling?

FEATHER BOWLING IS A GAME SIMILAR TO BOCCE BALL
WHERE THE TARGET IS A PIGEON FEATHER.

Bowling was even featured in many comics throughout
the years. In one installment of "Hi and Lois" from
1979, do you know who said, "I packed up my golf
clubs, my bowling shoes, the booze in my desk, and
quit"?

WHILE SITTING AT A BAR WITH HI, LONGTIME CHARACTER
THIRSTY TALKS ABOUT QUITTING HIS JOB.

Not to be outdone, the famous comic strip "Beetle
Bailey" talked about bowling. In a strip first run in
1984, General Halftrack brings his ball to the office to
brag about his high game. Do you know his score?

ALONG WITH THE BALL HE BROUGHT A BANNER TO BRAG
ABOUT HIS 285 GAME.

What Nascar driver hosted a tournament at a bowling
center across from the Indianapolis Motor Speedway to
benefit a children's hospital?

JEFF GORDON WAS THE HOST AT AMF RACEWAY LANES.

Dallas Mavericks owner Mark Cuban once bowled in a
PBA Pro-Am. Can you name the tournament?

THE PBA DAYS INN OPEN.

In 1991, what personality starred in a bowling comedy video called "Life in the Bowling Lane"?

THIS UNRATED VIDEOTAPE STARRED "THE UNKNOWN COMIC."

If you were going to bowl in a tournament and needed to clean your bowling ball, why would you not use acetone, kerosene, or denatured alcohol?

BECAUSE THEY ARE NOT APPROVED CLEANERS FOR BOWLING BALLS AS PUBLISHED BY THE ABC/WIBC.

If someone told you they were thinking of baking their bowling ball you might think they were crazy. However, someone came up with logic for this controversial idea. Why would anyone think of baking their bowling ball?

IF YOU HAVE A REACTIVE RESIN BOWLING BALL, THE VERY CHARACTERISTIC OF THE SHELL MAKES IT SOAK UP A LOT OF OIL. THEREFORE, SURFACE CLEANING OR EVEN SANDING DOES NOT PROPERLY CLEAN THE BALL. SOME PEOPLE HAVE HAD SUCCESS BY PLACING THEIR BOWLING BALL IN A LOW HEAT OVEN AND WIPING THE OIL AS IT OOZES TO THE SURFACE. [AUTHOR'S NOTE: DO NOT TRY THIS AT HOME! TAKE IT TO YOUR LOCAL PRO SHOP TO BE PROPERLY CLEANED.]

Dave Letterman lists his favorite record albums of all time. What title earned a listing in *The New Bowling Trivia Book*?

THE CELEBRITY BOWLING CHRISTMAS ALBUM.

The musical celebrity known as Lil' Kim was once quoted in *Rolling Stone* magazine in reference to bowling. Can you repeat this rather interesting quote?

"I HAVEN'T HAD SEX IN EIGHT MONTHS. TO BE HONEST, I NOW PREFER TO GO BOWLING."

It's True! After reviewing and researching hundreds of bowling related websites this one had to be included. Any ideas of which site wins my award as the strangest bowling related website?

THE OFFICIAL BOWLING BALL HEAD NANNY WEBSITE.

Bowling hustlers sometimes use illegally weighted bowling balls to gain an unfair scoring advantage. They drill holes in balls and fill them with a heavy substance. These are called Dodo balls. What would you be referring to when discussing a 7-9 Dodo ball?

UNSCRUPULOUS BOWLERS WOULD CEMENT HALF OF A SEVEN-POUND BALL TO A HALF OF A NINE-POUND BALL. THE RESULTING BALL WOULD "CLIMB" INTO THE POCKET.

What was the betting line the first time a Las Vegas casino accepted bets on a Professional Bowlers Association event?

FOUR-TO-ONE ODDS WERE GIVEN THAT PETE WEBER WOULD WIN.

In what year were these odds offered?

1985.

How many games are bowled each day around the globe?

OVER SEVEN MILLION GAMES ARE BOWLED EACH DAY.

On average, how many visits do American bowlers make to bowling centers each year?

LEAGUE BOWLERS AVERAGE 30 VISITS EACH YEAR WHILE CASUAL BOWLERS AVERAGE 11 VISITS PER YEAR.

Prior to the advent of electric hand dryers, what was used to dry bowlers' hands between deliveries?

A TOWEL WAS TIED TO THE END OF THE BALL RACK. MANY TIMES THEY WERE NOT CHANGED BETWEEN MATCHES.

What famous radio broadcaster endorsed youth bowling in the late 1950s?

PAUL HARVEY, WHO WAS IMPRESSED AFTER A VISIT TO A BOWLING CENTER WITH HIS SON.

What is the world record for stacking bowling balls on top of each other?

IN 1989, THE RECORD OF NINE WAS SET. HOWEVER, THIS RECORD WAS BROKEN IN NOVEMBER OF 1998 BY DAVID KREMER, WHO STACKED 10 BALLS ON TOP OF EACH OTHER.

What are the odds that you will bowl a 300 game on your next attempt?

11,500 TO ONE.

A bowling center with the unique name of El Jebowl will always have bragging rights regarding a famous celebrity who bowled there. Any ideas who?

PRINCESS DIANA AND HER SONS WILLIAM AND HARRY BOWLED THERE. HER BOWLING BALL AND SHOES ARE DISPLAYED IN THE BOWLING CENTER ALONG WITH THEIR SCORE SHEET.

In the late fifties, The Bowling Proprietors Association of America produced some posters featuring a clown called "Bowlzo." These posters were designed to be displayed in bowling centers to deliver a message. What message were they trying to deliver?

BOWLZO WAS A GOOFY CLOWN THAT VIOLATED EVERY RULE OF BOWLING ETIQUETTE PICTORIALLY. HOPEFULLY, THIS WOULD STIMULATE PROPER ETIQUETTE ON THE LANES.

In what country will you find the world's largest bowling center?

JAPAN.

How many lanes does this bowling center have?

THE NAYOGA #2 GRAND BOWLING CENTER HAS 156 LANES. THE TOKYO WORLD LANES CENTER, NOW CLOSED, HAD 252 LANES.

McCook Bowl in Dayton, Ohio was considered a marvel of engineering because of what reason?

THIS BOWLING CENTER HAD 44 LANES WITHOUT A VERTICAL SUPPORT POST IN THE BOWLING LANE AREA.

Pin Boy Tidbits

1. In October of 1954, what well-known magazine wrote a negative article about bowling titled "The Sport That Ruins Youngsters?"

2. Many vagabonds found jobs as pinsetters. Even though the money was not very good, what made this an attractive job for many transients?

3. During the 1950s, masking units began appearing in bowling centers everywhere. Besides looking good aesthetically, what was another purpose for masking units?

4. By 1960, what had most U.S. bowling centers done?

5. In 1944, the U.S. government clamped down on bowling proprietors and demanded that all pin boys obtain one of these. What did the government require?

6. From 1939 to 1944 there were 24 reported bowling alley fires throughout the U.S. Ten of these started under similar circumstances. What did these 10 fires have in common?

6. ALL WERE DETERMINED TO HAVE BEEN STARTED BY THE CARELESS SMOKING OF PIN BOYS.

5. ALL PIN BOYS HAD TO OBTAIN SOCIAL SECURITY CARDS.

4. REPLACED PIN BOYS WITH AUTOMATIC PINSETTING EQUIPMENT.

3. THEY SERVED THE PURPOSE OF HIDING THE OFTEN "SURLY" PIN BOYS.

2. FACED WITH A SHORTAGE OF PINSETTERS, MANY BOWLING PROPRIETORS PROVIDED LODGING FOR PINSETTERS.

1. REDBOOK MAGAZINE. THE STORY DISCUSSED PROBLEMS INVOLVING PIN BOYS.

A bowling pin car is on display at the National Bowling Hall of Fame. It was built for promotional purposes by an Ohio bowling proprietor in the early 1940s. What make of automobile was the foundation for this unique vehicle?

A STUDEBAKER.

How much money was the owner of the car offered for its purchase and the accompanying patent rights?

IN EXCESS OF $10,000.

The Bowling Pin Car has a license plate that shouldn't surprise you. What does this plate say?

GO-BOWL.

In 1943, you could purchase a product, through the bowling magazines, intended for league secretaries. It cost one dollar. What was this essential product that was years ahead of its time?

THE "ALL PURPOSE BOWLING CALCULATOR" COULD FIGURE INDIVIDUAL AVERAGES FROM 61 TO 220.

What are the requirements to be eligible for PBA membership?

BOWLERS MUST HAVE AN AVERAGE OF AT LEAST 200 OVER THE PREVIOUS TWO 66 GAME MINIMUM SEASONS. BOWLERS WHO AVERAGE AT LEAST 190 IN AN ABC OR WIBC SANCTIONED SPORT LEAGUE ARE ALSO ELIGIBLE TO JOIN.

In Russia, if you stopped by the Orlenok Hotel you could visit their bowling center. If you wanted to bowl for an hour, how much would it cost?

486 RUBLES UNTIL 6 P.M. AND 780 RUBLES THEREAFTER.

Thousands of bowlers participate in Moonlight Doubles, in which they bowl in a darkened environment. In 1943, the Franklin House Bowling Alley had an early version of this concept. The only illumination in the building was at the scoring tables and the pin end of the alleys. Keeping with the times, what did they call their tournament?

A "BLACKOUT TOURNAMENT." EVEN THE PIT LIGHTS WERE SHADED WITH RED CLOTH.

During the 1940s, you could buy a product called Shaafco Bowling Sandals. What was the purpose of these sandals?

THEY WOULD TAKE THE PLACE OF BOWLING SHOES BY BEING WORN OVER STREET SHOES WHILE BOWLING.

In August of 1944, *Bowling Magazine*, the official publication of the American Bowling Congress, featured a cover of past winners of various ABC tournaments. While this in itself was not unusual, what did each member of this featured group have in common?

THEY WERE ALL MEMBERS OF VARIOUS BRANCHES OF THE MILITARY.

If you visited Bend, Oregon, why would you find 300 bowling balls on Gene Carsey's farm?

BECAUSE HE HAS THE LARGEST BOWLING BALL GARDEN IN THE WORLD.

While you are there, what related items could you purchase?

HE SELLS BOWLING BALL SEEDS.

What is the median age of a bowler in the U.S.?

THE MEDIAN AGE OF A RECREATIONAL BOWLER IN THE U.S. IS EARLY TO MID TWENTIES, WHILE THE MEDIAN AGE OF A LEAGUE BOWLER IS EARLY TO MID FORTIES.

There were 42 straight years of American Bowling Congress Tournaments before they were postponed. What led to the three-year postponement of this tournament?

WORLD WAR II.

Throughout the years, the American Bowling Congress passed many rules and regulations. In 1909, what did the ABC demand that each bowling team bring to the ABC tournament?

EACH TEAM HAD TO BRING AT LEAST ONE BOWLING BALL.

Another rule that passed in 1924 was a prohibition against gambling-related companies. These companies were not allowed to do what?

THEY COULD NOT SPONSOR BOWLING TEAMS.

In 1928, gambling was prohibited in league and tournament bowling by the ABC. What punishment could participants caught violating this rule expect?

THEY COULD BE BARRED FROM COMPETING BECAUSE OF "MORAL DELINQUENCIES."

In 1933, gold, silver, and bronze rings were offered for the first time by the ABC for award scores. What type of awards were issued prior to the 1933 season?

BEFORE 1933, ONLY MEDALS WERE GIVEN AS AWARDS.

What function did a product known as the Bowler's Bucket serve? It even came with a three-fingered grip.

IT WAS AN ICE BUCKET IN THE SHAPE OF A BOWLING BALL.

What professional bowler spent four days in Vietnam visiting servicemen as part of a goodwill tour of the Orient?

DICK WEBER.

One bowling center holds the record for most sanctioned leagues in one center. This occurred in the 1970-71 season. Can you name the center and the city where it is located?

SOUTHLAND LANES, IN FLINT, MICHIGAN, HAD 120 SANCTIONED LEAGUES IN THE 1970-71 SEASON.

What professional female bowler worked part-time along with her daughter setting pins?

MARION LADEWIG.

Super Seniors

1. A lot of people can bowl a score of twice their age. In fact, it does not sound that difficult. How old was Mollie Marler of Missouri when she bowled a score exactly twice her age?

2. This could be one of the great feel-good bowling stories of all time. Ted Byram of Vero Beach, Florida bowled a perfect game at the age of 82. Now, this in itself is a grand accomplishment. What else made this a unique and special perfect game?

1. SUPER SENIOR MOLLIE WAS 101 YEARS OLD WHEN SHE BOWLED A 202 GAME IN 1985.

2. MR. BYRAM ACCOMPLISHED HIS PERFECT GAME JUST 17 DAYS AFTER SUFFERING A MINOR STROKE. HIS PREVIOUS BEST GAME WAS A 280.

In the autumn of 1942, a 10-team league was organized in Detroit. There was a specific criteria for joining this league. What was it?

> THIS LEAGUE WAS ESTABLISHED FOR LEFT-HANDED BOWLERS ONLY.

Many people remember the famous headline that read "Dewey Defeats Truman" for the U.S. Presidential election. What connection did Thomas Dewey have to bowling?

> AS GOVERNOR OF NEW YORK, HE WELCOMED ALL PARTICIPANTS OF THE 1946 ABC TOURNAMENT IN BUFFALO, NEW YORK.

History tells us that the U.S. Army had a top-secret program to develop an atomic bomb that was called the Manhattan Project. What could bowling possibly have to do with this nuclear project?

> IN OAK RIDGE, TENNESSEE, A BRAND NEW EIGHT-LANE BOWLING CENTER WAS BUILT FOR THE INHABITANTS OF THIS CITY, WHO WERE QUARANTINED FROM LEAVING THE DEVELOPMENT BECAUSE OF SECURITY REASONS.

In Oak Ridge, also known as Atomic City, what action did bowlers take shortly after their bowling center was built?

> THEY FORMED THEIR OWN CITY BOWLING ASSOCIATION.

As the A-bomb program expanded, how many total bowling centers were built for the inhabitants of the secret cities used in the atomic project?

> FOUR BOWLING ESTABLISHMENTS WITH A TOTAL OF 36 LANES.

One of the earliest known bowling competitions in France was a winner-take-all tournament. What entry fee did each participant have to supply?

> A CHICKEN. THE WINNER WOULD RECEIVE ALL THE CHICKENS.

That's nothing. Tournaments in Germany and Poland around the year 1500 also paid prizes in livestock. What did the winner receive in each country?

> IN GERMANY THE PRIZE WAS A DEER, WHILE IN POLAND THE WINNER TOOK HOME AN OX.

In July 1902, a magazine for women called the *Delineator* advised women to take up bowling for what reason?

> THE MAGAZINE STATED, "A FEW HOURS OF BOWLING EACH WEEK WILL DO A WOMAN FULLY AS MUCH, IF NOT MORE GOOD THAN ANY OTHER FORM OF EXERCISE."

In December 1981, the Jim Beam Distillery offered to donate a portion of the proceeds from the sale of their commemorative pin decanters to a specific cause. What did this donation benefit?

THE CONSTRUCTION OF THE NATIONAL BOWLING HALL OF FAME.

Brunswick pinsetters are used throughout the world. Can you name this unique location of two lanes with Brunswick pinsetters, where theology students reportedly use them constantly?

IN THE BASEMENT OF THE VATICAN.

It is not documented whether Pope John Paul II has used these bowling lanes, but he has participated in this bowling variation. What game has he tried?

BOCCE.

The Fourth Frame:

For the Record!

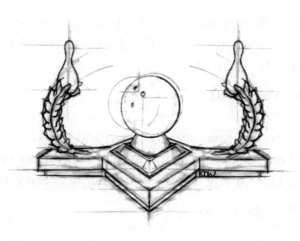

How many consecutive "Brooklyn" strikes did Mary Sharp of Akron, Ohio knock down enroute to her 300 game?

MARY ROLLED 11 STRAIGHT BROOKLYNS BEFORE GETTING A POCKET HIT STRIKE ON HER LAST BALL IN THE TENTH FRAME.

Who was the first ambidextrous individual to bowl sanctioned 300 games both right-handed and left-handed?

NEIL BAYES OF ST. LOUIS. HIS FIRST CAME RIGHT-HANDED ON DECEMBER 5, 1963 AND LEFT-HANDED ON JUNE 20, 1970.

What is the highest sanctioned three-game series that includes at least one game below 200?

A 799, BOWLED BY DON HARTLEY, FEATURED GAMES OF 300, 199, AND 300.

The record for consecutive duplicate games, or games of the same score, by an individual is eight. What was the repetitive score?

A SCORE OF 202 IN 1988.

Talk about shotmakers. Two men and one woman were able to consecutively string together a number of spares. How many did they successfully convert?

THIRTY IN A ROW.

Accomplishing an 800 series is still a significant bowling event. Do you know the gentleman that holds the record for most career sanctioned 800 series?

JOHN CHACKO OF PENNSYLVANIA HAS TALLIED 54 800 SERIES IN HIS CAREER.

Emory Krauthoefer from Milwaukee did something in his league for 61 consecutive years. You won't believe this one.

MR. KRAUTHOEFER WAS HIS LEAGUE'S SECRETARY FOR 61 YEARS.

While every bowler dreads the 7-10 split, it is even worse when you get them in back-to-back frames. Why didn't that bother Victor Morra of Connecticut in 1999?

HE CONVERTED BOTH SPLITS IN CONSECUTIVE FRAMES.

Many bowlers strive for a perfect 300 game. Joe Norris held the record at 86 years of age for many years. That record has been broken. Who broke it and how old was the gentleman?

JOE DEAN IN 1999 AT THE AGE OF 87 YEARS, 6 MONTHS, AND 5 DAYS.

Mr. Norris, a tremendous ambassador of bowling, did set another record with his perfect game. What was it?

HIS 67 YEARS BETWEEN PERFECT GAMES IS THE LONGEST SUCH SPAN.

While we're talking about super seniors, Ed Tomek of Avon Park, Florida holds the record for highest three-game series for a senior. What was his series total?

AN 877 IN 1993.

Carl Chavez of Albuquerque, New Mexico should have been devastated when he was left with four consecutive 6-7-10 splits. How many of these splits did he convert into spares?

ALL FOUR.

Mr. Bret Dal Santo of Georgia must have been elated when he bowled his 887 series. However, he did set an interesting record. Do you know what it is?

WITH GAMES OF 299, 289, AND 299 HE BOWLED THE HIGHEST SERIES WITHOUT A 300 GAME.

Dominic Scruci of Philadelphia could be called Mr. Consistency for accomplishing this feat five times in a row. What record did Dominic set during league play in 1943 that still stands today?

HE BOWLED FIVE CONSECUTIVE THREE-GAME SERIES OF 618.

The next time one of your bowling teammates calls at the last minute to say they can't make it, remind them of Nellie Marsura of Washington state. How many years did she bowl in her league without an absence?

FORTY-THREE YEARS.

Four men have each bowled at least two 800 series in competition. What is unique about the men that put them in the record books?

THEY WERE AMBIDEXTROUS, AND EACH BOWLED AN 800 USING EACH HAND.

Mr. Si Hewitt had a busy season in 1976-77. What did he do nineteen different times each week?

BOWLED IN 19 DIFFERENT LEAGUES.

Mike Randesi, Jr. and Paul Cannon were bowling against each other in 1977 when they each bowled an 800 series to put them in the record books as the first opponents to do so. What else was unique about their accomplishment?

EACH WAS IN THE THIRD POSITION IN THEIR RESPECTIVE LINEUPS. IN 1997 THEY WERE JOINED BY VICTOR CORBIN, JR. AND ROB BARTON WHO KNOCKED DOWN 1625 PINS BETWEEN THEM WHILE BOTH BOWLING IN THE FIFTH SPOT.

Linda Lunsford of Seattle enjoyed the holiday season in 1993 because of what consecutive bowling record?

SHE BOWLED SIX CONSECUTIVE 700 SERIES IN HER LEAGUE BEGINNING IN DECEMBER 1993.

Audrey Gable of Allentown, Pennsylvania bowled a 300 game the evening of April 30, 1988. What was unique about this event?

AUDREY WAS APPROXIMATELY EIGHT MONTHS PREGNANT AT THE TIME.

Josey LaRocco of Louisville, Kentucky is the youngest male to record a 300 game. He did so at the ripe old age of 10 in 1998. Who was the youngest female to accomplish this feat?

NICOLE LONG OF ILLINOIS BOWLED HER 300 GAME IN 1995 AT THE AGE OF 12 YEARS, FIVE MONTHS.

Al Laureys and his wife Mazey were the first husband and wife to bowl 300 games. Al bowled his in 1962, while Mazey accomplished hers a year later. Both were right-handed. Who were the first left-handed husband and wife to bowl 300 games?

GERI AND DICK BEATTIE.

Sue Peterson has bowled 8 perfect games in her career. However, her husband, Rory, has a few of his own. How many 300 games has this husband and wife team put in the record books?

FORTY-ONE.

In 1953, Bill Phillips of Houston, Texas bowled a 300 game. Even though many had accomplished 300 games previously, what made this one unique?

IT WAS THE FIRST 300 GAME RECORDED ON AUTOMATIC PINSETTING EQUIPMENT DURING LEAGUE PLAY.

From 1996 through 1998, Rit Szczepanski of New York achieved a record that is truly remarkable. What did he do 88 times in a row?

HE BOWLED 88 CONSECUTIVE 200 GAMES.

Who bowled the first sanctioned 900 series in history?

JEREMY SONNENFELD FROM LINCOLN, NEBRASKA IN 1997. SINCE THEN, FOUR OTHERS HAVE ACCOMPLISHED THIS FEAT.

Roger Evans' average was 127 on April 12, 1991. Sometimes, everything goes your way. What did Roger accomplish that night?

HE HAD THE LOWEST AVERAGE OF ANY MALE BOWLER TO ROLL A 300 GAME.

During the 1932-33 season, Edward Mullen averaged 192. He did so, however, without accomplishing one of these. What was it?

EDWARD AVERAGED 192 WITHOUT BOWLING A 600 SERIES. HIS HIGHEST THAT SEASON WAS 599.

Ninety-two year old Joe Norris made history by tying an all-time ABC Tournament record of 71 tournaments attended. During those tournaments, he knocked down 123,770 pins. Can you name another active bowler who has knocked down more than 100,000 pins in ABC tournament appearances?

DICK WEBER WITH MORE THAN 102,000 PINS.

Ron Bahr from Topeka, Kansas became the first bowler in 100 years of American Bowling Congress Championship Tournament history to bowl back-to-back 300 games. The second and third games of his series were perfect, what was his first game score?

237 FOR AN 837 SERIES.

The Fifth Frame:

A Tough Time on the Lanes

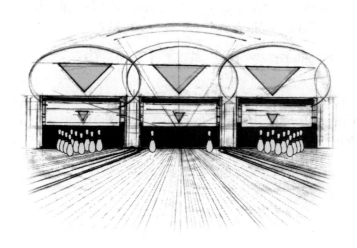

What is the lowest three-game sanctioned series that includes a perfect 300 game?

IN 1989, REED TOWNLEY OF ALABAMA RECORDED GAMES OF 89, 87, AND 300 FOR A 476 SERIES.

Think your team is in a rut? How many times did the De Snyder Plasterettes team of Port Huron, Michigan use the same team lineup?

FORTY-ONE YEARS.

John Prehm of New York holds the sanctioned record for the lowest game score in which a person bowled 11 strikes. What was his record-setting score?

TWO HUNDRED FORTY. JOHN BEGAN WITH THREE STRIKES, TOOK A ZERO IN THE FOURTH FRAME, AND THEN STRUCK OUT.

Splitsville? How many consecutive 7-10 splits did Payne Rose of St. Louis throw in 1962?

PAYNE THREW SIX CONSECUTIVE 7-10 SPLITS.

Before you feel too sorry for Payne, how many consecutive splits did Shirley Tophigh throw in Las Vegas during the 1968-69 season?

FOURTEEN STRAIGHT.

But even 14 straight pales in comparison to the number of splits that the Lengel Meat Packers men's team bowled during one game in 1955. Care to guess?

THIRTY-SEVEN SPLITS IN ONE GAME.

How about splits in one season? In 1978-79 Dean Bainer of Ohio bowled a record number of splits. Can you guess this amount?

HE HAD 213 SPLITS AS AN INDIVIDUAL.

How many consecutive ninepin counts did Pete Bland of Washington roll in 1976? (At least they weren't splits.)

EIGHTEEN NINEPIN COUNTS.

The dreaded gutter ball. Mary Ellen Handley of Florida bowled the highest game on record that includes a gutter ball. What was Mary Ellen's score?

290 DURING THE 1980-81 SEASON.

Two men and two women have tied each other by scoring the highest game without a single spare or strike. What milestone score did they achieve without the benefit of a single mark?

90.

Everyone talks about pins over average. What is the record for pins under average for one game?

> ANTHONY DELAHANTY OF ARIZONA ROLLED A 62 GAME WHILE CARRYING A 214 AVERAGE, FOR AN UNDER-AVERAGE SCORE OF 152.

Fouls happen to most bowlers occasionally, but what are the most fouls scored in one league game by an individual?

> BUD MATHIESON COMMITTED 15 FOULS IN ONE GAME IN 1946. HE CONTINUED THAT PACE AND WOUND UP WITH 37 FOULS DURING HIS THREE-GAME SERIES.

A Ladies Team bowling in a league in Indiana has the most consecutive losses in team play. You have to love their perseverance while you guess how many losses?

> THE "PEANUTS" TEAM LOST 132 IN A ROW.

The 4-6-7-10 split is sometimes knows as double pinochle. Mr. Alvin Hunter must hate this split after setting the record for most consecutive. Any guesses?

> MR. HUNTER HAD 4 CONSECUTIVE IN 1960. HOWEVER, HERMAN EAGLER HAD 5 IN ONE GAME.

You will not believe the lowest game in sanctioned league play. Think low.

> MIKE KAPPA FROM RACINE, WISCONSIN HOLDS THE RECORD OF "2."

How did PBA bowler Mark Baker
get the nickname "Moon?"

You will never guess the popular city in which
this "mooning" incident occurred.

WHILE BOWLING ON NATIONAL
TELEVISION DURING A TOURNAMENT,
HIS PANTS SPLIT, REVEALING HE
WASN'T WEARING ANY UNDERWEAR.
MIAMI.

Poor Richard Caplette of Connecticut managed to
throw 19 gutter balls in one game in 1971. How many
of these were consecutive?

ALL OF THEM. HE THREW NINETEEN CONSECUTIVE
CHANNEL BALLS ENROUTE TO HIS SINGLE-GAME RECORD.

If your bowling team is struggling to reach the 500
mark, consider the Men's Bible Class team from
Pennsylvania. What is unique about their team's 1957-
58 season?

THEY FINISHED THE SEASON WITH A COMBINED TEAM
RECORD OF ONE WIN AND 139 LOSSES.

The 7-10 split receives a lot of notoriety, but the 8-10 is also very difficult. What is the record for the most 8-10 splits in one three-game series?

> John Ermi must have wanted to quit the game when he was credited with twelve 8-10 splits in 1937.

Lynne Santucci of New York was depressed when she bowled an 87 in the 1971-72 season. What score did she get on her next game?

> 299 for a 212 pin margin between games.

Harvey Lemons of Florida did not have split trouble. In fact, he bowled nine strikes during his game. However, he recorded the lowest sanctioned game bowled that included nine strikes. What was his score?

> Harvey bowled a 184.

The Sixth Frame:

Variations

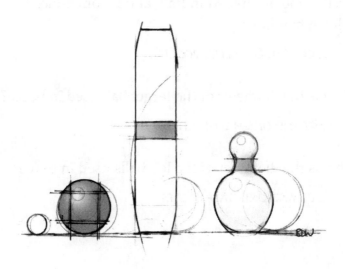

Skittles is a bowling game derived from which French game?

QUILLES.

In skittles, the wooden pins are also known as skittles. What is the wooden or rubber ball used in skittles referred to?

THE CHEESE.

How many pins are used in the game of skittles?

NINE.

In skittles, in what geometric shape are the pins placed?

A DIAMOND.

What game originated in Italy and is sometimes known as lawn bowling?

BOCCE (ALSO SPELLED BOCCIE).

What is the diameter of the target ball used in bocce?

ONE AND ONE-HALF INCHES.

What is the diameter of the lob balls used in bocce?

FOUR AND ONE-HALF INCHES.

Kayles was an early version of bowling. In Kayles, a ball was not used to knock down pins. What was used?

STICKS OR CLUBS WERE USED TO KNOCK DOWN PINS.

Cloish was a game almost identical to Kayles except for one major difference. Do you know the basic difference between Kayles and Cloish?

A BALL REPLACED THE STICKS OR CLUBS TO KNOCK DOWN PINS.

Time for an easy question. Do you know the name of the sport played primarily in Canada that is sometimes referred to as "ice bowling?"

CURLING.

What game is being referred to when the "bowler" is attempting to throw the ball past the batsman to score points? (While doing this, the "bowler" cannot have bent elbows.)

THE BRITISH GAME OF CRICKET.

Around 1540, the King of England granted licenses to certain gentlemen entitling them to play the game of skittles. What were the criteria for obtaining one of these licenses?

ONLY GENTLEMEN WITH HIGH INCOMES COULD RECEIVE A LICENSE.

Throughout the 1600s, ninepins was very popular. However, there were still many variations of the types of bowling games played. What country was known to have more types of bowling games than any other?

FRANCE.

In early variations of skittles, a kingpin was often part of the game. Why was a kingpin different than all other pins?

IN MANY CASES, A KINGPIN WOULD BE TALLER AND ALSO WORTH MORE POINTS THAN ANY OF THE OTHER PINS.

Another variation during the early days of bowling was known as Loggats. This game was extremely popular at sheep shearing festivals. What was unusual about the game of Loggats?

PARTICIPANTS USED ANIMAL BONES TO KNOCK DOWN PINS.

Q-Bowl was a table game version of tenpin bowling that was manufactured in Ohio. How did players of Q-Bowl knock down the miniature pins?

THEY SHOT A CUE BALL USING A BILLIARD CUE ACROSS A TABLE TO KNOCK DOWN MINIATURE BOWLING PINS.

In 1960, the Spare Time home bowling game was introduced. This game featured a magic slate score pad and cost only two dollars. What did this game utilize in place of bowling pins?

SPARE TIME WAS A DICE GAME IN WHICH EACH DIE REPRESENTED A BOWLING PIN.

Match the Bowling Term with its Definition

Washout

Greek Church

Anchor

Big Four

Turkey

Baby Split

      Last bowler in lineup

      2-7 or 3-10 leave

      4-6-7-10 leave

      4-6-7-8-10 or 4-6-7-9-10 leave

      Three strikes in a row

      1-2-10, 1-2-4-10, 1-3-7, 1-3-6-7 leaves

ANCHOR - LAST BOWLER IN LINEUP; BABY SPLIT - 2-7 OR 3-10 LEAVE; BIG FOUR - 4-6-7-10 LEAVE; GREEK CHURCH - 4-6-7-8-10 OR 4-6-7-9-10 LEAVE; TURKEY - THREE STRIKES IN A ROW; WASHOUT - 1-2-10, 1-2-4-10, 1-3-7, 1-3-6-7 LEAVES.

What was the name of a home version bowling game created by the Wilson Sporting Goods Company in 1942? Why was it unique?

DART-BOWL WAS A HOME VERSION BOWLING GAME THAT WAS UNIQUE BECAUSE PLAYERS THREW DARTS AT A BOWLING DARTBOARD TO SCORE POINTS.

In the 1960s, the Bally Company manufactured a pinball machine based on the game of bowling. What was the name of this pinball machine?

BOWL-O.

When the game of Duckpins was created in Baltimore around 1900, the balls used in competition were six inches in diameter. What is the diameter of a modern ball used in the game of duckpins?

FOUR AND SEVEN-EIGHTHS TO FIVE INCHES IN DIAMETER.

How did Duckpin bowling get its name?

JOHN MCGRAW AND WILBERT ROBINSON REMARKED THAT THE LITTLE PINS RESEMBLED FLYING DUCKS. THIS WAS PICKED UP IN A LOCAL NEWSPAPER STORY AND THE NAME STUCK.

One of the first ever Duckpin bowling centers was called the Diamond. What was unique about this establishment?

IT WAS A COMBINATION BAR, GYMNASIUM, AND TENPIN BOWLING ALLEY.

A brief explanation of Duckpin Bowling:

THE GAME IS SIMILAR TO TENPINS EXCEPT THE BALL IS ABOUT 5 INCHES AND THE PINS ONLY STAND 9.406 INCHES TALL. THE GAME WAS ESTABLISHED IN BALTIMORE IN THE YEAR 1900. SCORING IS SIMILAR TO TENPINS. YOU STILL GET A STRIKE IF YOU KNOCK DOWN ALL OF THE PINS ON YOUR FIRST BALL. KNOCKING THEM DOWN WITH TWO BALLS IS A SPARE. HOWEVER, IN DUCKPINS YOU ARE GIVEN A THIRD BALL THAT ALLOWS YOU TO COUNT ADDITIONAL PINS IF YOU DO NOT GET A STRIKE OR SPARE. THE HIGHEST POSSIBLE SCORE IS 300 AND HAS NEVER BEEN ACHIEVED DURING SANCTIONED EVENTS. THE CURRENT HIGH SCORE FOR MEN IS 279 AND 265 FOR WOMEN.

The governing body of Duckpins is the National Duckpin Bowling Congress based in Maryland.

A brief explanation of Candlepin Bowling:

FIRST PLAYED IN 1880, THE SPORT OF CANDLEPINS IS UNIQUE TO NEW ENGLAND AND THE CANADIAN PROVINCES. THE GAME IS A SKILLED SPORT THAT DEMANDS GREAT TIMING WHILE REQUIRING MINIMAL PHYSICAL STRENGTH. THE GAME USES PINS THAT ARE 15 AND ¾ INCHES HIGH, 2 AND 15/16 INCHES WIDE IN THE CENTER AND TAPERING DOWN ON EACH END. BALLS ARE 4½ INCHES IN DIAMETER AND WEIGH NO MORE THAN 2 POUNDS, 7 OUNCES. THERE ARE TEN FRAMES AND YOU ROLL THREE BALLS IN EACH FRAME UNLESS YOU SCORE A STRIKE OR A SPARE. THE FIRST PUBLISHED HIGH SCORE IN 1880 WAS 112. MOST AVERAGE SCORES WERE IN THE 80s. RALPH SEMB HAS THE HIGHEST SINGLE GAME RECORD SANCTIONED SCORE FOR MEN WITH 245, WHILE GLENNIS HICKEY TOPS THE WOMEN WITH A HIGH SCORE OF 202.

A brief explanation of 5 Pin Bowling:

IN 1905, CANADA'S FIRST REGULATION TENPIN LANES WERE SET UP IN DOWNTOWN TORONTO. THE ESTABLISHMENT'S OWNER, TOMMY RYAN, REACTED TO CUSTOMER COMPLAINTS ABOUT THE GAME BEING STRENUOUS. HE HAD HIS FATHER REDUCE THE SIZE OF THE PINS TO APPROXIMATELY ¾ OF THEIR ORIGINAL SIZE. HE THEN SPACED FIVE OF THESE PINS EQUALLY ON THE TENPIN TRIANGLE. AFTER ADDING A SMALLER FIVE INCH, 3½ POUND BALL, IN EFFECT THE GAME OF 5 PINS WAS BORN. SEVERAL CHANGES HAVE TAKEN PLACE OVER THE YEARS. NOTABLY, A RUBBER BAND WAS ADDED TO THE PINS IN 1912. A PERFECT GAME IN 5 PINS IS 450. A CANADIAN GOVERNMENT REPORT PRODUCED IN 1995 STATED THAT THERE WERE 521,000 REGULAR 5 PIN BOWLING PARTICIPANTS.

The Seventh Frame:

Stars and Strikes

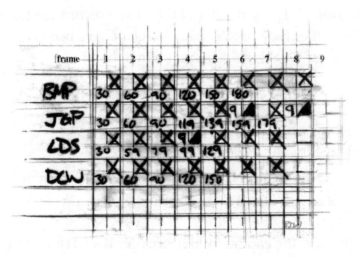

On March 2, 1985, which professional bowler lost one million dollars by only four pins on national television?

PETE WEBER.

Why was he in the position to win a one million dollar bonus?

HE NEEDED TO WIN ALL THREE NATIONAL TOURNAMENTS SPONSORED BY THE MILLER BREWING COMPANY. HE HAD WON THE FIRST TWO TOURNAMENTS BEFORE LOSING IN THE FINAL MATCH OF THE THIRD.

Who defeated Weber in the title match to ruin his million-dollar payday?

ERNIE SCHLEGEL.

The Bowling Writers Association of America voted Marion Ladewig Bowler of the Year a record ten times. Two other lady professional bowlers have been honored four times. Can you name them?

WENDY MACPHERSON AND DONNA ADAMEK.

Who was the first person to bowl a 300 game on television?

GRAZ CASTELLANO IN 1953 WHILE BOWLING FOR THE KRUEGER BEER TEAM.

Who was the captain of the Krueger Beer Team at the time?

ANDY VARIPAPA.

In 1946, Andy Varipapa won the All Star Tournament (today's U.S. Open). How old was he when he became the national champion?

FIFTY-FIVE YEARS OLD.

Who was the first man to ever repeat as national champion?

ANDY VARIPAPA.

While Mr. Varipapa earned his way into the ABC Bowling Hall of Fame with back-to-back victories, another bowler who dominated bowling during the 1950s is considered by many to be the greatest bowler who ever lived. Can you name him?

DON CARTER.

Mr. Carter had a unique nickname that referred to his unorthodox crouching approach. What was this nickname?

THE ST. LOUIS SHUFFLER.

Don Carter's success earned him many things including one special distinction that no other athlete in history had done before him. Do you know what?

MR. CARTER WAS THE FIRST ATHLETE TO SIGN A MILLION DOLLAR CONTRACT.

Can you name the famous bowling company that gave him this lucrative deal to promote their equipment?

EBONITE.

Bowling Magazine, the official magazine of the American Bowling Congress, began selecting All American teams in 1956. This practice continues to this day. In only one year were the five members of the All American team from one city. Can you guess the bowlers and the city they were from?

IN 1963, DON CARTER, DICK WEBER, BILLY WELU, RAY BLUTH, AND HARRY SMITH WERE ALL FROM ST. LOUIS.

Between 1981 and 2002, one member of the PWBA won the earnings title a record six times. Which lady professional won this title in 1983, '84, '85, '86, '93, and 1994?

ALETA SILL. ALETA ALSO WON PWBA PLAYER OF THE YEAR IN 1984 AND WAS VOTED BWAA BOWLER OF THE YEAR IN 1984 AND '85.

Walter Ray Williams, Jr. is a star by any measure on the PBA Tour. He was named PBA player of the year in 1986, '93, '96, '97, and 2003. He is also a six-time World Champion in another sport. Can you name the sport?

HE IS A SIX-TIME WORLD CHAMPION IN HORSESHOE PITCHING. HE IS ALSO A THREE-TIME JUNIOR WORLD CHAMPION IN HORSESHOE PITCHING.

He was elected to the NHPA Hall of Fame for his horseshoe prowess in 1988. In what year was he elected to the PBA Hall of Fame?

1995.

Who were the first three bowlers in the Professional Bowlers Association to earn more than $100,000 in a single year?

EARL ANTHONY, MARK ROTH, AND MARSHALL HOLMAN.

In the 1990s, '80s, and '70s, male and female bowlers have been named Bowlers of the Decade by various bowling periodicals. Can you name them?

1990s	**Lisa Wagner**
	Mike Aulby
1980s	**Betty Morris**
	Earl Anthony
1970s	**Tish Johnson**
	Walter Ray Williams, Jr.

1970s—MORRIS, ANTHONY
1980s—WAGNER, AULBY
1990s—JOHNSON, WILLIAMS, JR.

Two very capable lady pros hold the record for most pro titles won in a season. Can you name them?

PATTY COSTELLO WON 7 TITLES IN 1976 AND CAROLYN DORIN-BALLARD REPEATED THIS ACCOMPLISHMENT IN 2001.

In 1989 this lady professional from Detroit set a PWBA record for consecutive strikes. Any idea on the number?

CHERYL DANIELS SET THE RECORD WITH 29 CONSECUTIVE STRIKES IN ALBUQUERQUE, NEW MEXICO.

Chris Schenkel and Nelson "Bo" Burton, Jr. were the announcing team for the PBA Tour on television for many years. Who was the color commentator that Bo Burton replaced?

BILLY WELU.

On July 1, 1982, what bowler astounded the bowling world with three perfect games, the first perfect 900 series recorded in 87 years?

GLEN ALLISON.

How many sanctioned 300 games had Glen Allison bowled prior to the night of this astounding performance?

FOUR. HOWEVER, HIS RECORD 900 WAS NOT A RECOGNIZED SERIES.

What was the name of the bowling center in which
Glen Allison bowled his perfect series?

LA HABRA 300 BOWL IN CALIFORNIA.

Glen bowled his 900 series while competing in a trio
league. While much has been said about Glen's three-
game series, what were the three-game series totals for
each of his teammates on this historic night?

564 AND 467.

On March 12, 1958, the famous Budweiser Team
bowled a then-record 3858 series. Name the two
members of this team who bowled perfect 300 games
enroute to this score.

RAY BLUTH AND TOM HENNESSEY.

Can you name the remaining members of the famous
Budweiser team?

DON CARTER, DICK WEBER, AND PAT PATTERSON.

What leading money winner on the PBA tour
discovered the "soaker" and used it to his advantage?

DON MCCUNE, WHO DISCOVERED THAT BY SOAKING A
PLASTIC BOWLING BALL IN A CHEMICAL SOLUTION, THE BALL
WOULD HAVE MORE TRACTION ON THE LANES.

What year was Don McCune the leading money winner and how much did he win?

IN 1973 HE WON $67,000.

PWBA bowler Wendy Macpherson holds the record for career earnings with $1,194,535.00. Do you know who is in second place?

ALETA SILL WITH $1,071,194.00 IN EARNINGS.

Who was the first winner of the Inaugural High Roller Tournament in Las Vegas?

MICK MORTON.

How much did Mick Morton win in that first High Roller?

$210,000.

Talk about strength and perseverance, what PWBA bowler competed in 236 consecutive tournaments?

TISH JOHNSON. SHE IS ALSO THIRD ALL-TIME IN CAREER EARNINGS.

What PBA bowler used to stick his sore thumb in a potato to help it heal?

DON JOHNSON.

In 1977, Mark Roth won four PBA titles and more than $100,000 on the tour in prize money. How much did he win his first year on the PBA tour?

A LITTLE OVER $1,000.

What was the first year the Pro Bowler's Tour was televised on Saturday afternoons?

1962.

Chris Schenkel was the longtime voice of the Saturday afternoon telecast of the Pro Bowler's Tour. Name two movies in which Chris had acting roles.

CHRIS APPEARED IN *REQUIEM FOR A HEAVYWEIGHT* AND *NATIONAL VELVET.*

Hank Marino was given a unique honor by the National Bowling Writers Association. His string of victories in the '20s and '30s gave him a unique distinction as a top bowler. What was the honor bestowed on him?

THE WRITERS DUBBED HANK THE "BOWLER OF THE HALF CENTURY."

What Hall of Famer was later voted the "greatest of all time"?

DON CARTER IN 1970.

Speaking of Mr. Carter, how many times was he Bowler of the Year?

SIX TIMES. 1953, 1954, 1957, 1958, 1960, AND 1961.

Famous bowler Ned Day had an unusual superstition. What was it?

HE WOULD NOT SHAKE HANDS WITH ANYONE FOR FEAR OF INJURING HIS BOWLING HAND.

Who were the first father and son duo to be elected to the American Bowling Congress Hall of Fame in the Performance category?

NELSON BURTON, SR. AND NELSON BURTON, JR.

In 1959, how much money did the leading money winner on the professional bowlers tour earn?

DICK WEBER WON $7,672.

How much did the leading money winner on the professional tour earn in 1993?

WALTER RAY WILLIAMS, JR. WON $296,370.

What PBA member holds the record for the most 200 games in succession?

IN 1993, WALTER RAY WILLIAMS, JR. BOWLED 61 CONSECUTIVE 200 GAMES IN TOURNAMENT PLAY.

Bowling for Dollars

1. Who won the Inaugural Firestone Tournament of Champions in 1965, which featured a $100,000 prize fund?

2. What is the record for earnings won in a single PBA season?

1. Billy Hardwick, who won $25,000 for his first place finish.
2. Walter Ray Williams, Jr. demolished the old record held by Mike Aulby by winning $419,700 in 2002-03. Mike Aulby had won $298,237 in 1989.

What PBA member holds the record for most PBA tournament titles in one year?

MARK ROTH WON EIGHT TOURNAMENTS IN 1978.

Two other PBA members have each won seven tournaments in one year. Who are they?

WALTER RAY WILLIAMS, JR. IN 1993 AND EARL ANTHONY IN 1975.

In 1994, PBA member Norm Duke bowled the highest losing score on national television during a PBA tournament. What was his losing score?

280.

Who beat Norm Duke and what score did he bowl?

BRYAN GOEBEL SHOT 296 TO DEFEAT DUKE'S 280.

What PBA bowler was the first to bowl a perfect 300 game on national television during a PBA tournament?

JACK BIONDOLILLO IN AKRON, OHIO IN 1967.

What is the combined total of perfect games that Earl Anthony and Mark Roth have bowled on national television?

ZERO.

What PBA member had the highest single-season earnings while never winning a tournament?

PETE MCCORDIC WON $156,476 IN 1987.

Who bowled 14 consecutive years with at least one title on the PBA tour?

EARL ANTHONY (1970-83).

Who was the youngest player to win a PBA tournament?

NORM DUKE WAS JUST 18 YEARS OLD IN 1983.

Who was the oldest player to win a PBA tournament?

BUZZ FAZIO WAS 56 WHEN HE WON IN SACRAMENTO IN 1965.

What Hall of Famer won three of the first four PBA tournaments ever held?

DICK WEBER.

In what year was the first Senior PBA tournament held?

THE INAUGURAL SENIOR CHAMPIONSHIP WAS HELD IN 1981.

Who won the 1981 PBA Senior Championship?

ABC HALL OF FAMER BILL BEACH.

Earl Anthony holds the record for all-time PBA tournament wins with 41. Who is second?

WALTER RAY WILLIAMS, JR. WITH 37.

Which professional female bowler holds the career record for most PWBA title victories?

LISA WAGNER WITH 32. ALETA SILL IS IN SECOND PLACE WITH 31 TITLES.

At the end of the 2002 season, four women professional bowlers have eclipsed the one million dollar mark in career earnings. Can you name them?

WENDY MACPHERSON, ALETA SILL, TISH JOHNSON, AND LEANNE BARRETTE.

One of the most successful bowlers of all time is Earl Anthony. What other pro sport did Earl aspire to before trying the PBA tour?

> MR. ANTHONY HAD HIS SIGHTS ON BECOMING A LEFT-HANDED PITCHER IN MAJOR LEAGUE BASEBALL. AN ANKLE INJURY ENDED THIS HOPE.

What is the highest scoring televised championship match between professional female bowlers?

> FIVE HUNDRED FIFTY-FIVE PINS. LEANNE BARRETTE DEFEATED ALETA SILL 279 TO 276 IN 1988.

There was a higher scoring match between two PWBA bowlers. It occurred in Davie, Florida in the year 2000. Can you name the bowlers and their scores?

> MICHELLE FELDMAN AND KIM TERRELL BOTH BOWLED PERFECT 300 GAMES.

Johnny Petraglia, in 1971, and Mark Roth, in 1977, each won three consecutive professional bowling tournaments. What professional won three consecutive tournaments three different times?

> DICK WEBER IN 1959, 1960, AND 1961.

Seven women bowlers have won the U.S. Open Championship twice in their careers. Can you name the woman who has won this championship eight times?

> MARION LADEWIG.

After winning the national All Star Match Game tournament in Chicago, Ms. Ladewig won something beyond the cash prize. Any ideas?

> BESIDES THE PRIZE MONEY, MS. LADEWIG EARNED A PERSONAL APPEARANCE CONTRACT WITH BRUNSWICK. THIS ARRANGEMENT WENT ON FOR MORE THAN THIRTY YEARS.

In 1959 Marion Ladewig helped organize the Professional Women Bowler's Association. What happened during the following year?

> SHE WON THE PWBA'S INAUGURAL TOURNAMENT.

Who was the first woman bowler to earn $100,000 in a single season?

> LISA WAGNER WON $105,500 IN 1988.

In 1965, Dick Weber led professional bowlers with $47,675 in prize money won. During that same year, how much did the leading women's professional earn?

> BETTY KUCZYNSKI WON $3,792.

In 1983, Earl Anthony won the last of his record-setting six selections as PBA Player of the Year. Who was selected as the Professional Women's Bowling Association Player of the Year in 1983?

> LISA WAGNER.

In 1923, the Peterson Tournament paid out a total of $5,600 in prize money. How much did the first-place winner receive?

$2,000.

What was the individual entry fee for this tournament the following year?

$25.

The George London Dream Tourney was a unique bowling tournament that had a sizable prize fund in 1958. What was the total value of the prizes offered that year?

$50,000 IN 1958.

Johnny King won the Inaugural George London Tournament in Chicago in 1956. What were the criteria for entering this tournament?

YOU MUST HAVE BOWLED A PERFECT GAME IN ABC SANCTIONED COMPETITION WHILE WEARING A GEORGE LONDON BOWLING SHIRT.

The 1958 tournament offered an automobile as a prize. What type of automobile could you have won?

A PLYMOUTH BELVEDERE HARD TOP.

There is only one Father-Son duo in the PBA section of the Bowling Hall of Fame. Can you name them?

DICK WEBER AND HIS SON PETE WEBER.

At what age did Pete Weber first bowl a 300 game?

He was twelve.

Many people know that Dick Weber was one of the true ambassadors of the game. You really know bowling if you know what Dick did for a living before becoming a pro bowler.

He was a mailman.

Dick Weber accomplished countless feats during his storied career. Which of the following things did he not do?

A. Cashed in 72 consecutive tournaments

B. Bowled at a television set outdoors on the Letterman Show

C. Won tournaments in six separate decades

D. Converted 7-10 split on television

D. Dick did everything but convert the 7-10 split on TV.

Andy Varipapa was a terrific ambassador of bowling. What was his nickname?

"The Clown Prince of Bowling."

But it was not all fun and games for Andy. At age 55, Andy won a prestigious national tournament. Can you name the tournament?

IT WAS THE ALL STAR TOURNAMENT WITH A PURSE OF $1000. WHAT MAKES THIS ACCOMPLISHMENT EVEN MORE INCREDIBLE IS THAT IT TOOK OVER 100 GAMES TO WIN THIS TOURNAMENT. FOR GOOD MEASURE, ANDY WON IT THE FOLLOWING YEAR ALSO.

The Eighth Frame:

Equipment!

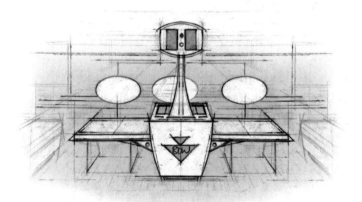

A modern bowling ball cannot exceed the maximum allowable weight of 16 pounds. What is the minimum allowable weight?

THERE IS NO MINIMUM.

Many modern bowling balls use this material as part of the core. Can you guess the material?

LIMESTONE.

Perhaps the most expensive bowling shoes made are a pair of Prada ladies red leather. What is the retail price of these fashionable shoes?

$430.00 FOR THE PAIR. HOWEVER, THAT DOES INCLUDE A TRAVEL BAG.

When referring to a model of designer sunglasses called "bowling," what designer marketed these fashionable specs?

CHRISTIAN DIOR.

Okay, you have the Prada shoes and the Dior sunglasses, what type of bowling bag should you purchase to complete your elegant ensemble?

YOU COULD BUY A BURBERRY BOWLING BAG FOR JUST $295.00.

In the modern game of bowling, 10 pins are arranged in a triangle. What is the distance between each pin?

EACH PIN IS 12 INCHES AWAY FROM THE NEXT PIN.

In the 1930s, many bowlers still used a two-hole bowling ball. One hole was for the thumb and one for the middle finger. While the three-hole ball was gaining in popularity, what was unique about a "slot ball"?

A SLOT BALL WAS A BOWLING BALL WITH ONE LARGE HOLE BIG ENOUGH FOR TWO FINGERS.

What two types of wood have been used extensively to manufacture bowling lanes?

MAPLE AND PINE.

What was the purpose of a "two way" bowling ball?

BETWEEN 1930 AND 1940, THIS HOUSE BALL HAD TWO DIFFERENT SIZED GRIPS THAT COULD BE USED BY EITHER MEN OR WOMEN.

What was the name of the very popular urethane bowling ball produced by AMF?
Hint: It was the winningest ball on the 1983 PBA tour.

THE ANGLE.

What was the unique color of Brunswick's first urethane bowling ball, The Edge?

IT WAS RED.

Any ideas on the name of the tremendously popular bowling ball that dominated the PBA Tour in 1977?

THE COLUMBIA YELLOW DOT.

What would have been the heaviest legal weight of a bowling ball in 1902?

EIGHTEEN POUNDS.

What was your 1902 vintage 18-pound bowling ball made of? (Here's a hint: *Lignum vitae* is the Latin term for this common substance.)

WOOD.

What type of bowling ball did Earl Anthony use when he became the first bowler to win $100,000 in prize money during a single season?

AN EBONITE MAGNUM VI.

What is the diameter of a modern bowling ball?

EIGHT AND ONE-HALF INCHES.

Many of you have seen different types of "clear" bowling balls with something embedded inside. All of the following items could be purchased inside of a clear bowling ball except one. Which item could you not purchase at press time?

A. A CLEAR BALL WITH 2 JACK DANIELS BOTTLES INSIDE.

B. A CLEAR BALL WITH AN EAGLE SITTING ON AN AMERICAN FLAG INSIDE.

C. A CLEAR BALL WITH A RED ROSE INSIDE.

D. A CLEAR BALL WITH A GARGOYLE INSIDE.

E. A CLEAR BALL WITH A CIGAR INSIDE.

E. ALL COULD BE PURCHASED EXCEPT FOR THE CIGAR.

The success of the Brunswick Corporation's rubber Mineralite bowling ball prompted the company to do what?

IN 1906 BRUNSWICK OPENED A NEW 100,000 SQUARE FOOT FACTORY IN MUSKEGON, MICHIGAN.

Everyone throws an occasional gutter ball. Knowing that the circumference of a bowling ball is approximately 27 inches, what is the depth of a lane gutter at its deepest point?

AT LEAST ONE AND SEVEN-EIGHTHS AT THE CENTER.

The bowling equipment manufacturer Qubica is known for its innovative equipment and exciting scoring graphics. How many bowling centers in the world have installed Qubica equipment?

MORE THAN 1400 CENTERS WORLDWIDE.

Where was the very first installation of Qubica equipment?

IN A FRENCH BOWLING CENTER DURING 1993.

On a bowling lane, there are several dots or aiming points between the foul line and the arrows. These are sometimes known as cherries. What is the total number of cherries on a bowling lane?

THERE ARE 10 DOTS OR CHERRIES SEVEN FEET FROM THE FOUL LINE.

In 1936, the Brunswick Corporation introduced their "20th Century" line of bowling equipment, which was colorful and streamlined. What standard piece of bowling equipment was this?

THIS WAS AN EARLY VERSION OF TODAY'S MASKING UNITS.

Before limestone, this material was used as a core for many bowling balls. What was it?

SAWDUST.

Many golfers are familiar with the durability of some types of golf balls. Can you name the surface material that is used on both golf balls and certain bowling pins?

SURLYN.

In 1923, for what price could you purchase a new Ebonite bowling ball?

THEY WERE $14 EACH WITH NO PRICE VARIATION FOR EITHER A TWO OR THREE-FINGERED BALL.

Bowling proprietors could purchase a set of 10 bowling pins for $5 in 1923. How much does a set of pins cost today?

IN EXCESS OF $100 PER SET OF 10.

How many aiming arrows are on a bowling lane?

SEVEN.

Let's not forget about bowling shoes. During the 1920s, what could you expect to pay for a pair of bowling shoes?

$4.65 PER PAIR.

The gutter sections located at the pin area of a bowling lane next to the pin deck are a unique shape in contrast to the rest of the gutters. What shape are they?

FLAT, AS OPPOSED TO CONCAVE.

What was the weight of the original robotic pinsetting machine?

TWO THOUSAND POUNDS.

In 1958, you could purchase men and women's broadcloth bowling shirts for $4.95 each. How much were these shirts if you chose to have them made of gabardine?

$6.95.

If you wanted to purchase a brand-new bowling ball in 1902, what would you have expected to pay?

ABOUT $4.25.

What was unique about the Triangle Sep-A-Rator bowling bag that set it apart from its competitors?

THIS BAG FEATURED A SEPARATE COMPARTMENT FOR YOUR BOWLING SHOES, AWAY FROM YOUR BOWLING BALL.

In 1958, a new piece of bowling equipment was introduced by the Chicago Hardware Foundry Company called a Sani-Dry. What was the purpose of the Sani-Dry?

> A SANI-DRY WAS A PATENTED ELECTRIC HAND DRYER THAT WAS MOUNTED ON THE BALL RETURNS.

What was the distinct shape of the Sani-Dry machine?

> IT RESEMBLED A BOWLING BALL.

The Brunswick Corporation reached a sales milestone in 1959. What piece of equipment had reached the pinnacle of twenty thousand sold by 1959?

> THEIR 20,000TH AUTOMATIC PINSETTER WAS INSTALLED IN A BOWLING CENTER IN CONNECTICUT.

Why would men bowling in the 1950s want to wear Don Carter Bowling Slacks?

> BECAUSE THEY HAD THE HIDDEN STRETCH WAISTBAND.

In 1966, a bowling accessory called a Tele-Strike was introduced that you could wear on your waist as you bowled. What was the intended purpose of this product?

> THIS $3.95 ITEM WAS DESIGNED TO GIVE YOU INSTANT FEEDBACK ABOUT WHAT YOU WERE DOING WRONG IN YOUR DELIVERY AND HOW YOU COULD CORRECT IT.

When wooden bowling lanes or alleys were first used, bowlers rolled the ball on a bare wood surface. Shellac was then used as a lane coating. What were the drawbacks of using shellac?

SHELLAC WAS VERY SOFT AND THE BALL TRACK AREA WORE OUT EVERY TWO TO THREE WEEKS. THEREFORE, RECOATING HAD TO BE DONE OFTEN, CHANGING THE LANE SURFACE.

What other types of lane finish followed the use of shellac?

LACQUER, URETHANE, WATER-BASED, AND SYNTHETICS.

In 1987, what Brunswick bowling ball went on to become the most popular in Brunswick history?

THE RHINO.

During the 1900s, cork balls were made of lightweight pressed wood. Composition balls followed these and were similar except for one variation. What improvements were made with a composition ball?

THEY WERE BASICALLY CORK BALLS COVERED WITH A HARD RUBBER COATING.

During the early years of outdoor bowling, bowlers often set their pins on wood slabs or flat stones. Later, three different substances were used to create smoother, more level lanes. What were the substances?

CLAY, CINDERS, AND SLATE.

A product that originated in Tennessee was called the "Alley Cat." This product reportedly eliminated the need to scrub the soles of bowling shoes with steel wool. What was the "Alley Cat?"

AN AUTOMATIC SHOE CLEANER DESIGNED FOR PLACEMENT WITHIN BOWLING CENTERS. JUST DROP FIVE CENTS IN THE COIN SLOT AND YOU RECEIVED 25 SECONDS OF CLEANING POWER.

Before electricity, what lighting method was used to illuminate bowling lanes?

GASLIGHTS.

Before the use of scoresheets, how did bowlers keep score?

SCORES WERE WRITTEN ON SLATE BOARDS WITH CHALK.

Chalk was also used in bowling alleys for another very different purpose. What other function did chalk perform in a bowling center?

BOXES OF CHALK WERE MOUNTED AT FLOOR LEVEL NEXT TO THE ALLEYS SO THAT BOWLERS COULD RUB THE SOLES OF THEIR SHOES IN IT TO IMPROVE TRACTION.

Why is a proactive resin ball sometimes known as a particle ball?

PROACTIVE RESIN BALLS WILL ACTUALLY HAVE SMALL PARTICLES OF CERAMIC, MICA, SILICA, OR RUBBER EMBEDDED IN THE SURFACE OF THE BALL.

Before ball returns were automatic, how did they work?

PIN BOYS WOULD SHOVE THE BALL DOWN A RAMP THAT WOULD END UP ON A RACK IN THE BOWLER'S AREA. PIN BOYS WHO WERE UNHAPPY ABOUT THE VELOCITY OF A BOWLER'S DELIVERY WOULD SOMETIMES RETURN THEM EXTRA HARD SO THEY WOULD FALL OFF THE RACKS.

Everyone knows that bowling balls made of wood were typical for awhile. After wood, can you list, in order of introduction, the other bowling ball materials?

HARD RUBBER, PLASTIC OR POLYESTER, URETHANE, REACTIVE RESIN, AND PROACTIVE RESIN.

Electronic foul detectors were a much-welcomed invention to the bowling industry. How were fouls determined before they were invented?

A FOUL JUDGE WOULD SIT ON A RAISED STOOL AND MANUALLY CALL FOULS ALONG HIS LINE OF SIGHT. AS YOU CAN IMAGINE, THIS SOMETIMES RESULTED IN HEATED ARGUMENTS.

A "Bowl Handl" (sic) was an amazing device that delivered a bowling ball without using the finger holes. Rubber suction cups were used to pick up the ball. In what year was this $80 product available?

1960.

The Kegeltron was also available in 1960. The Kegeltron was known as a "framemaster automatic totalizer." For what purpose was it used?

THE KEGELTRON WAS A MACHINE DESIGNED FOR BOWLING PROPRIETORS TO METER THE TOTAL AMOUNT OF FRAMES BOWLED DURING A BUSINESS DAY.

What is the circumference of a modern bowling ball?

MINIMUM CIRCUMFERENCE IS 26.704 INCHES, NOT TO EXCEED 27.002 INCHES.

How tall is a modern regulation bowling pin?

FIFTEEN INCHES.

In 1948 a new innovation was introduced that dramatically improved accuracy for bowlers. Do you know what this innovation was?

ARROWS AND DOTS WERE ADDED TO LANE BEDS BY THE BRUNSWICK CORPORATION. THIS GAVE BOWLERS ADDITIONAL AIMING POINTS.

The Ninth Frame:

Marketing

If you chose not to wear a George London shirt while bowling, you could choose a Service bowling shirt. What unique claim did a Service bowling shirt make?

THE SERVICE BOWLING SHIRTS CORPORATION EXPLAINED THAT THEIR SHIRTS WERE SANITIZED FOR LASTING FRESHNESS AND WERE THE BOWLING SHIRTS WITH THE BUILT-IN DEODORANT.

In a contemporary commercial for Miller Lite Beer, the punch line "stick em up, stick em up" is used. Where does the person who utters the punch line end up at the end of the commercial?

IN A BOWLING CENTER LOUNGE.

In 1954 all of the following companies had something in common: El Producto cigars, Wurlitzer music boxes, Ballantine, Budweiser, and Strohs Beer. Can you name it?

ALL WERE USING BOWLING AS A WAY TO DISPLAY THEIR PRODUCTS TO THE PUBLIC.

During the year 1963, baseball great Yogi Berra appeared in a publicity photo standing in a batter's box preparing to hit. Bowling star Buddy Bomar was the pitcher. Can you name the personality who was the catcher for this unique photo?

MARION LADEWIG WAS THE "STAR" CATCHER IN THIS PICTURE.

If you purchased a Brunswick lollipop ball, bag and matching shoe ensemble, what did that show?

THAT YOU HAD GOOD TASTE.

Who said bowlers weren't smooth. In a 1949 *Life* magazine ad featuring a man and woman bowling, what was the tagline for Barbasol Shave Cream?

"YOU'RE RIGHT DOWN MY ALLEY...WITH THAT SMOOTH BARBASOL FACE."

In another version of bowling being used to market a product, this ad features a woman holding a red bowling ball and wearing a bowling jacket. The front of her jacket says "strikers" and ran in *Road & Track* magazine in the late 1980s. What product was being advertised?

WINSTON CIGARETTES.

Fox Sports ran a television commercial with the tagline "Bowling would be better if it were hockey." Do you remember this commercial?

ONE WOMAN IS ON THE APPROACH AND STARTING HER DELIVERY. A SECOND WOMAN COMES OUT OF THE SETTEE' AREA, KNOCKS THE WOMAN DOWN AND SHE SLIDES INTO A DIFFERENT LANE.

What was the title of a bowling magazine widely distributed in Japan during the 1970s?

TOP BOWLER.

Why would anyone drop a bowling ball on a mattress?

IN A MARKETING CAMPAIGN FOR SIMMONS BEAUTYREST MATTRESSES, A BOWLING BALL IS DROPPED ON A BEAUTYREST MATTRESS THAT HAS A SET OF BOWLING PINS ON IT. WHEN THE BALL HITS, THE PINS DO NOT MOVE. THE TAGLINE THAT FOLLOWS: SIMMONS BEAUTYREST, THE DO-NOT-DISTURB MATTRESS.

The AMF corporation produced a Michael Jordan Slam Ball. What unique feature did this bowling ball have?

MICHAEL'S NUMBER 23 COULD BE FOUND OUTLINED BY A BASKETBALL.

Mickey Rooney, Alice Fay, Ginger Rogers, and Ronald Coleman were all pictured bowling together in the 1940s. What was the occasion of this star-studded bowling event?

MGM STUDIOS SPONSORED A BOWLING PARTY.

What bowling ball manufacturer's advertising slogan was "the ball that bowls right?"

EBONITE.

Even the heavy metal band Metallica can be connected to bowling. In fact, you could purchase a Metallica King Nothing Bowling Shirt. What was embroidered on the back of this retro '50s style bowling shirt?

ON THE BACK WERE THE WORDS "KING NOTHING LANES" AND IT FEATURED 3 BOWLING PINS.

In 1925, how much would you expect to pay for home delivery of a national bowling magazine?

FIVE CENTS PER WEEK FOR 52 WEEKS.

If you owned a Brunswick-Balke-Collander Mineralite bowling ball, what did their advertising claim?

USING THEIR EQUIPMENT ESTABLISHES YOU AS A LEADER.

What major liquor company produced a glass liquor decanter in the shape of a bowling pin?

IN 1958, THE JIM BEAM DISTILLERY PRODUCED THESE COLLECTIBLE DECANTERS TO DISTRIBUTE THEIR BOURBON.

In 1933, what transportation company used the advertising jingle, "Merrily we bowl along...to the tournament or anywhere?"

GREYHOUND LINES.

Can you name two different Nascar drivers who were featured on commemorative bowling balls?

JEFF GORDON AND DALE EARNHARDT.

In 1941, the magazine *The Woman Bowler* included an advertisement for a bowling ball that was called "The Ball of Champions!" Who was the manufacturer of this ball?

THIS CAME FROM THE BOWLING BALL DEPARTMENT OF THE MANHATTAN RUBBER MANUFACTURING CO.

The Miller Brewing Company has had an ongoing relationship with bowling.

1. During one bowling-themed television commercial, a bowler is pictured working up a sweat in a bowling center. What is the bowler doing?

2. In another notoriously funny Miller commercial, a young man enters a bowling center and asks for a size 8 rental shoe. The counter attendant only has one pair left. Do you remember the size of the remaining pair?

There was a series of commercials starring the Miller Lite All Stars. Can you answer the following questions about the first Lite Beer Bowling Tournament?

3. What Hall of Fame bowler is seated at the scoring table?

4. Famous football player Deacon Jones utters a bowling quote. What was it?

5. What Miller Lite All Star has to throw the final ball in the tournament?

6. In the final scene of this commercial, what former football coach breaks through the backdrop complaining about not getting his turn?

6. John Madden.
5. Comedian Rodney Dangerfield throws the last ball and when it hits the pins, the ball bounces off without knocking any down.
4. "Deacon's my name and bowling's my game."
3. Don Carter.
2. They were a size 19.
1. He was manually cleaning his bowling ball because the automatic ball cleaning machine was out of order.

What company's advertisement advised bowlers to "Get in the groove and stay there with 33 to 1?"

PABST BLUE RIBBON BEER, WHICH WAS BLENDED FROM 33 FINE BREWS.

In 1958, what baseball-star-turned-bowling-proprietor endorsed Brunswick Automatic Pinsetters?

NEW YORK YANKEE GREAT, YOGI BERRA.

What WWF star's image could be found on a Brunswick Viz-a-Ball bowling ball?

THE ROCK.

What was the name of Yogi Berra's bowling center that was located in New Jersey?

BERRA-RIZZUTO BOWLING LANES, WHICH YOGI CO-OWNED WITH PARTNER AND FELLOW BASEBALL PLAYER, PHIL RIZZUTO.

During the Christmas gift-giving season of 1958, what was included with the purchase of any Ebonite Tornado or Satellite bowling ball?

FREE GIFT WRAPPING THAT INCLUDED CRIMSON COLORED RIBBON.

By now everyone knows that Brunswick produced the Mineralite bowling ball. What was the name of the Brunswick ball produced and marketed for women?

IT WAS CALLED A WHELANITE.

If you drank a beverage that was advertised as "The perfect way to top your game," what would you be drinking?

FALSTAFF BEER.

Clorox Bleach also wanted to show its connection to bowling. A *Good Housekeeping* magazine ad featuring five ladies wearing all white bowling uniforms ran in June of 1964. What type of bowling ball is featured in the ad?

ONE OF THE TEAM MEMBERS IS HOLDING A BLUE BRUNSWICK CROWN JEWEL BALL. HER BOWLING SHIRT IS EMBROIDERED WITH THE NAME ROSE.

In December of 1941, *Photoplay* magazine featured yet another bowling ad showing lady bowlers with the caption "Keep Going in Comfort." Which of the following products was being advertised?

A. SUPP-HOSE BOWLING SOCKS

B. LADIES DELIGHT BOWLING SHOES

C. FIBS KOTEX TAMPONS

D. DR. SCHOLLS FOOT POWDER

C. THE ANSWER IS FIBS KOTEX TAMPONS.

What breakfast cereal featured a "Bowling Champions" contest that you could win by submitting a finishing verse to a bowling jingle that was on the box?

WHEATIES, THE BREAKFAST OF CHAMPIONS.

What was the top prize for winning the Wheaties contest?

$20,000.

In July of 2002, the Verizon wireless company announced the availability of new technologies. What were they?

THEY ANNOUNCED THE AVAILABILITY OF DOWNLOADABLE GAMES FOR CELL PHONES THAT INCLUDED JAMDAT BOWLING AND JAMDAT BASEBALL.

Hall of Fame bowler Billy Welu offered personal bowling instruction by mail in 1960 for $4.98 post paid. What type of instruction would you receive?

YOU WOULD HAVE RECEIVED IN THE MAIL A 33-1/3 LP RECORD BY MR. WELU ENTITLED "STRIKE."

A 1945 print ad for Kentucky Tavern Whiskey shows a strong association with bowling. Kentucky Tavern was known as the Aristocrat of Bonds. What helped identify this product with bowling?

IN THE AD, TWO COASTERS WITH BOWLING PINS ARE DISPLAYED ALONG WITH A BOWLING BALL LIGHTER AND A BOWLING PIN CIGARETTE HOLDER.

What bowling ball advertised in the 1960s was said to have "Thrust" and also that "extra mix"?

COLUMBIA 300.

The Ebonite bowling ball company advertised in the 1960s that a chemical put "Steam" in the ball you roll. What substance was included in their bowling ball formula?

SULPHUR.

If you went to your local bowling pro shop and asked for a Warhol, what would you be looking for?

A BRUNSWICK VIZ-A-BALL BOWLING BALL WITH AN ANDY WARHOL INSPIRED COKE BOTTLE DESIGN.

During a television commercial for PCS Vision from Spring, what celebrity is seen standing in a bowling center while wearing a bowling shirt?

LITTLE RICHARD.

Bowling is not only used to market products, but is also featured in public service spots. Two bowlers named Al and Sarah are featured in a bowling center while Al bowls a strike. Can you name the organization that is represented in this media ad?

THE AMERICAN CANCER SOCIETY.

The Tenth Frame:

Miscellanea

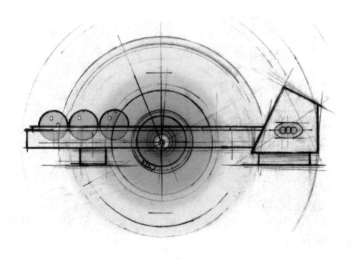

How much did Detroit bowler Therm Gibson win for throwing six consecutive strikes in 1961 while bowling on the television show "Jackpot Bowling"?

GIBSON WON $75,000. AS AN EXAMPLE OF HOW LARGE A PAYOUT THIS WAS, GARY PLAYER WAS THE LEADING MONEY WINNER ON THE PRO GOLF TOUR THAT YEAR. HE WON $64,540.00 FOR THE ENTIRE SEASON.

If you visited eBay in April of 2003 and entered the word bowling, how many items would be for sale?

A. 390

B. 779

C. 1400

D. 5279

D. THE ANSWER IS 5279 ITEMS FOR SALE ON 4/19/03.

What was listed that day for the bargain price of $325,000.00?

A 14-LANE BOWLING CENTER IN STUTTGART, ARKANSAS.

What does the PBA Tour give to its top 70 bowlers every year, that is a first for any sports organization?

STOCK OPTIONS.

What Olympic gold medalist was a spokesperson for bowling in 1985?

MARY LOU RETTON.

What world-famous artist was commissioned $50,000 to paint a bowling-themed portrait?

> LEROY NEIMAN WAS THE ARTIST OF "THE MILLION DOLLAR STRIKE."

What PBA Hall of Fame bowler is depicted bowling on this painting? Who else appears?

> EARL ANTHONY. FELLOW HALL OF FAMERS ANDY VARIPAPA, DON CARTER, AND NELSON BURTON, JR. ARE ALSO FEATURED IN THE BACKGROUND.

Where is the original painting now on display?

> AT THE NATIONAL BOWLING HALL OF FAME IN ST. LOUIS, MISSOURI.

On what date was the groundbreaking ceremony for the National Bowling Hall of Fame held?

> APRIL 20, 1982.

What well-known sports arena is located across the street from the National Bowling Hall of Fame?

> BUSCH STADIUM.

Which future U.S. President was featured on the cover of *Bowler's Journal* magazine in 1946? His wife appeared with him. Who was she?

> RONALD REAGAN APPEARED WITH FIRST WIFE, JANE WYMAN.

Which left-handed U.S. President was featured on the cover of *The National Kegler* magazine in 1947?

PRESIDENT HARRY TRUMAN.

This gentleman pro bowler was one of the first bowlers to write an instruction book on the sport. *How to Bowl* was a huge success. Who wrote this book?

NED DAY.

How to Bowl was the first sports instruction book to use what as a teaching method?

SEQUENCE PHOTOGRAPHY.

Even after the Brunswick Company became synonymous with bowling, they still manufactured non-bowling related products. In 1912, they introduced a product that went on to sell 120,000 units per year. Any guesses what that product was?

AMERICA'S FIRST RUBBER TOILET SEAT.

Why would a bowling lane be considered Blocked?

A LANE WOULD BE BLOCKED IF IT WERE DELIBERATELY DRESSED TO INCREASE SCORING POTENTIAL.

If you were participating in a tournament and heard the term "all events," what would that mean?

ALL EVENTS IS A TOTAL SCORE FROM YOUR TEAM, DOUBLES, AND INDIVIDUAL EVENTS.

If you were accused of throwing a back up ball, what would that indicate?

THAT THE BALL HOOKED TOWARD THE HAND THAT DELIVERED IT. FOR EXAMPLE: IF YOU BOWLED LEFT-HANDED AND THE BALL MOVED TO THE LEFT, IT WOULD BE CONSIDERED BACKING UP.

If you threw a crossover strike, what would another term for that feat be?

BROOKLYN.

How can a bowling pin be a messenger?

A PIN THAT ROLLS ACROSS THE LANE AND TAKES DOWN ANOTHER PIN IS REFERRED TO AS A MESSENGER.

What is it called when a bowler does not get a spare or a strike in a frame?

THAT FRAME IS CONSIDERED AN OPEN FRAME.

What is another term for a gutter ball?

A CHANNEL BALL.

What is a Dutch 200 game?

A SCORE RESULTING FROM ALTERNATING SPARES AND STRIKES WITH A SCORE OF TWENTY IN EACH FRAME.

Which pin is sometimes known as the kingpin?

THE FIVE PIN.

What is spot bowling?

AIMING AT A SPOT, A MARK ON THE LANES, OR EVEN A SPECIFIC LANE BOARD INSTEAD OF AIMING AT THE PINS.

What is a Jersey strike?

ANOTHER NAME FOR A BROOKLYN STRIKE.

What is considered dead wood?

DOWNED PINS THAT REMAIN ON A LANE AFTER A HIT ARE CALLED DEAD WOOD.

Dick Weber has traveled the world promoting bowling. He has put on demonstrations in many unique places, including intermissions at rodeos. None may have been as unusual as his promotional match against women's champion, Sylvia Wene. Where was this match located?

ON BOARD A JET AIRPLANE IN FLIGHT.

Mr. Hockey, Gordie Howe, has a unique connection to bowling. Any guesses?

GORDIE AND HIS WIFE COLLEEN MET AT THE "LUCKY STRIKE," WHICH WAS A BOWLING ALLEY LOCATED ON GRAND RIVER AVENUE IN DETROIT, MICHIGAN.

If you were playing Alley 19, what would you be doing?

YOU WOULD BE PLAYING A SIMULATED BOWLING GAME ON YOUR COMPUTER.

Comedy Central has a unique approach to a bowling show. If you have ever seen "Let's Bowl," you will remember it. Name the two men who do running commentary during the show.

CHOPPER AND WALLY.

Music to Bowl By

1. "It's music to a bowler's ears" is the slogan of what bowling product?

2. Can you name the pro bowler who is the featured singer on two of the songs?

3. Which of the following is not a song featured on "Bowl Me Over"?

A. "LET THE GOOD TIMES ROLL"

B. "BEER FRAME BLUES"

C. "FOUR STEP APPROACH"

D. "YOUR LOVE IS LIKE A 7-10 SPLIT."

4. Can you name the professional woman bowler who is featured on her own CD entitled "Dreams"?

4. CHERYL DANIELS DEMONSTRATES HER VOCAL TALENTS ON THIS CD. CHERYL PREVIOUSLY HAS SUNG AS A BACKGROUND SINGER WITH MARTHA AND THE VANDELLAS.

3. D WAS NOT ON THE CD.

2. PBA BOWLER RANDY PEDERSON IS FEATURED ON VOCALS.

1. A MUSIC CD CALLED "BOWL ME OVER," WHICH FEATURES TEN SONGS INSPIRED BY BOWLING.

Competitors participating in "Let's Bowl" have more than just a ball in their arsenal. What can they do if they utilize the distraction option?

THEY CAN SNEAK UP BEHIND THEIR OPPONENT AND BLOW AN AIR HORN WHILE THEY TRY TO BOWL. [AUTHOR'S NOTE: I KNOW A LOT OF LEAGUE BOWLERS WHO WOULD LIKE TO DO THAT TO THE "SLOW-BOWLER" IN THEIR LEAGUE.]

In 1964, the Brunswick Corporation formed a division to operate bowling centers. BRC or Brunswick Recreation Centers went on to operate how many bowling centers by 1965?

MORE THAN 130 BOWLING CENTERS.

If you were bowling on a MiniLane, how would that be different from a standard bowling lane?

THE MINILANE IS A SPECIAL BOWLING UNIT THAT FITS INTO A FOOTPRINT THAT IS LESS THAN HALF THE SIZE OF A PAIR OF TRADITIONAL TENPIN BOWLING LANES.

By now you know that there is tenpins, duckpins, candlepins, etc. But what in the heck is the sport of pin shooting?

PIN SHOOTING HAS GROWN IN POPULARITY AT GUN RANGES AND CLUBS THROUGHOUT THE UNITED STATES. IT IS A TYPE OF SHOOTING MATCH. GENERAL GUIDELINES USE FIVE STANDARD BOWLING PINS SET ON A TABLE 25 FEET FROM THE SHOOTER.

The names Fusion, BlueFire, Fantasy X, and Mirage sound like Generation X nightclubs. But really, they all have one thing in common. What is it?

THEY ARE ALL BOWLING BALL NAMES.

Do not miss this classic video entitled *Nude Bowling* released in 1995. The plot involves a celebrity bowling tournament. What is unique about the participants in this tournament?

THEY ARE NUDE EXCEPT FOR SOCKS AND BOWLING SHOES.

The History Channel offered a unique look at bowling through its "Stories from the Hall of Fame – Bowling" programming. What PBA star narrated this informative program?

PARKER BOHN.

If you happened to visit the website BowlingShirt.com, you would find their unique motto. Any guesses?

"MAKING THE WORLD A BETTER PLACE ONE BOWLING SHIRT AT A TIME."

Many people by now have seen the hit movie *Shrek*. When you purchase the DVD there are some ancillary programs provided. Which one relates to bowling?

"FAIRY TALE LANES" IS A ROUSING GAME OF ELF BOWLING.

Match the following bowling terms with their meaning:

Dime store

Double wood

Soldier

Open

A hidden pin directly behind another.

A frame without a mark.

When one pin is directly behind the other.

The 5-10 split

Only one of the following names is a real website. Can you pick the correct one?

A. YUCATAN BOWLING

B. BOWLING HERE, THERE, EVERYWHERE

C. BOWLING FOR JESUS

D. GEOMETRIC BOWLING

The following is a list of computer bowling games. Please match the game with the year it was introduced.

Brunswick Circuit Pro Bowling	1995
Flintstones Bedrock Bowling	1996
PBA Bowling	1997
Ten Pin Alley	1998
Animaniacs: Ten Pin Alley	2000

1. DIME STORE - 5-10 SPLIT; DOUBLE WOOD - ONE PIN DIRECTLY BEHIND ANOTHER; SOLDIER - ONE PIN HIDDEN BEHIND ANOTHER; OPEN - FRAME WITHOUT A MARK
2. C. YES, THERE IS A WEBSITE ENTITLED BOWLING FOR JESUS
3. CIRCUIT PRO - 1998; FLINTSTONES - 2000; PBA BOWLING - 1995; TEN PIN ALLEY - 1997; ANIMANIACS - 1996

The great sports writer Grantland Rice has a specific connection to bowling. What is it?

HE PRODUCED A NINE-MINUTE DOCUMENTARY TITLED *BETTER BOWLING* IN 1942.

Of course everyone remembers the famous animated cartoon pair of Tom and Jerry. In a classic eight-minute cartoon released in 1942, Tom and Jerry find themselves in a bowling alley. What was the title of this Hanna-Barbera comedy short?

BOWLING ALLEY-CAT.

In the terrific year of 1958, a bowling book was released by Junie McMahon and Murray Goodman. What was the title?

MODERN BOWLING TECHNIQUES. THIS HARDCOVER OFFERED INSTRUCTION AND INCLUDED PHOTOS.

The following year, 1959, introduced another instructional book titled *Guide to Natural Bowling*. The book was prepared by Victor Kalman. What was Mr. Kalman's title?

VICTOR KALMAN WAS THE BOWLING EDITOR OF *SPORTS ILLUSTRATED*.

Which of the following is not an actual book title?

A. *Pearl and May at the Bowling Alley*

B. *Revolutions*

C. *Irma the Flying Bowling Ball*

D. *My Life in the Gutter*

D. *My Life in the Gutter* was not a published title.

Bowling Tips

Grip

Of the three basic grips in bowling, the conventional grip is recommended for beginners and is widely used by most average bowlers.

A bowler should choose a ball so the hand fits into the ball without gripping it too tightly or stretching the hand in order to hold the ball.

Stance

Position of the feet is a key factor of the stance. If a bowler is right-handed, the left foot should be extended forward a bit, perpendicular to the foul line. Left-handers, do the opposite. The knees should be slightly bent. The shoulders should be square to the foul line and the body should lean forward slightly.

The bowling ball should be held somewhere between the knees and chin, at the point that is the most comfortable for the bowler. The weight of the ball should be in the non-bowling ball hand.

What the bowler does in the stance will affect all other movements made up to the point of delivery. The entire process must be fluid, from stance to follow-through.

Approach

A four-step approach is recommended for beginners. Left-handers must reverse these left-right directions:

- Start with the right foot. At the same time, push the ball away, keeping it to the right side of the body so that a straight backswing and forward swing will result.

- The second step, made with the left foot, is at the point when the ball is at the bottom of the backswing.

- The third step, made with the right foot forward, is also the time when the ball is at the height of the backswing. Keep the shoulders square, and lean toward the foul line.

Delivery

The delivery is getting the ball from the bowler's hand to the pins. Do not drop the ball or throw it. Gently lay it down on the lane from three to twelve inches from the foul line.

At the point of releasing the ball over the foul line, the bowler should find his/her fingers in the ball and the thumb out. The thumb MUST come out first for a proper release. To give the ball a spinning action, a slight lift of the fingers should be made upon release.

The delivery hand should continue up in a hand shaking position for a correct follow-through.

Scoring

These are the symbols that make up the bowling shorthand:

A game consists of ten frames. Each box on the scoresheet represents one frame.

1	2	3	4	5	6	7	8	9	10
9 /	9 —	☒	☒	5 /	7 —	☒	6 —	8 /	☒ /
19	28	53	73	90	97	113	119	139	159

Two balls are bowled in each frame unless a strike is rolled. A strike occurs when all ten pins are knocked down with the first ball of the frame. All ten pins knocked down with the two allotted balls of the frame constitutes a spare.

If the bowler fails to knock down all ten pins with two balls, simply record the total number of pins downed, and add the total to the score for the previous frame.

1	2	3	4	5	6	7	8	9	10
9 /	9 —	☒	☒	5 /	7 —	☒	6 —	8 /	☒ /
19	28	53	73	90	97	113	119	139	159

If the bowler strikes, the score for that frame is TEN plus the number of pins knocked down by the next TWO balls.

1	2	3	4	5	6	7	8	9	10
9 /	9 −	X	X	5 /	7 − X	6 −	8 /	X	X
19	28	53	73	90	97	113	119	139	159

If the bowler spares, the score is TEN plus the number of pins knocked down with the FIRST ball in the next frame.

If a strike is made in the 10th frame, the bowler must roll two additional balls. For a spare in the 10th frame, the bowler rolls one extra ball. The maximum number of balls allowed in the 10th frame is three.

1	2	3	4	5	6	7	8	9	10
9 /	9 −	X	X	5 /	7 − X	6 −	8 /	X	X
19	28	53	73	90	97	113	119	139	159

The score is carried forward in each frame and the tenth will show the bowler's final score.

Spares

A bowler can roll as high as 190 without ever getting a strike, if all spares are made. The important factor in making a spare is the ANGLE. Spares should be shot from the opposite side of the approach—if a spare is to the right, stand to the left, and if the spare is to the left, stand to the right.

HEAD PIN SPARES are shot from the strike position. Adjust the angle of the approach depending on the combination of pins in the spare.

TWO PIN SPARES such as the 6-10 or 1-3 are made by aiming between the two pins. When the pins stand directly behind one another, such as the 2-8 or 3-9, a good solid hit on the front pin is essential. In all spares it is important to hit as many pins as you can with the ball, rather than knocking the pins into each other.

Splits

A split occurs when after rolling the first ball, at least two pins remain standing that are not adjacent to each other, with the head pin down.

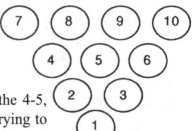

FIT-IN SPLITS, such as the 4-5, 5-6, 7-8, 9-10, are made by trying to fit the ball between them. Aim and timing are important there.

BABY SPLITS, such as the 2-7, or 3-10, are made by shooting cross-angles, aiming for the space between the pins.

Wider splits, such as the 5-7 or 4-10, can be made by sliding the 4 or 5 pin across into either the 7 or 10 pin. It is good strategy to shoot for one pin when you have splits such as the 7-10, 8-10, or the 4-6.

Etiquette

- Remember, a five-member team is allocated 45 minutes to complete ONE GAME. Avoidable delays hurt your team and all other bowlers scheduled behind you.

- Respect the equipment. Wait for the pinsetting machine to complete its cycle before releasing your ball. LOFTING THE BALL HURTS YOUR GAME AND DAMAGES THE LANE.

- Good bowling requires concentration. Provide your fellow bowlers the same courtesy you desire when it is your turn to bowl.

- When two people are ready to bowl on adjoining lanes, the bowler on the RIGHT has the right of way to bowl first.

Bowling Companies and Associations

American Blind Bowling Association (ABBA)
315 N. Main St.
Houston, PA 15342
(724) 745-5986

American Bowling Congress (ABC)
5301 S. 76th St.
Greendale, WI 53129-1127
1-800-514-BOWL
(414) 421-6400 / FAX: (414) 421-1194
www.bowl.com

American Wheelchair Bowling Association (AWBA)
2912 County Woods Lane
Palm Harbor, Florida 34683-6417
(727) 734-0023
www.awba.org

Billiard & Bowling Institute of America (BBIA)
200 Castlewood Dr.
N Palm Beach, FL 33408
(561) 842-4100 / FAX: (561) 863-8984

Bowling Proprietors' Association of America (BPAA)
615 Six Flags Dr.
Arlington, TX 76011
(817) 649-5105 / FAX: (817) 633-2940
www.bowl.com

Brunswick Corporation
One North Field Court
Lake Forest, IL 60045
(847) 735-4700 / FAX: (847) 735-4765
www.brunswick.com

Canadian 5 Pin Bowler's Association
1161-B Cyrville Rd.
Gloucester, ON K1J7S6
(613) 744-5090 / FAX: (613) 744-2217

Canadian Tenpin Federation
530 Home St.
Winnipeg Manitoba, Canada R3G 1X7
(204) 783-7453 / FAX: (204) 783-4856
www.tenpin.org/ctf.html

Federation Internationale des Quilleurs (FIQ)
1631 Mesa Ave. Ste. A
Colorado Springs, CO 80906
(719) 636-2695 / FAX: (719) 636-3300
www.fiq.org

High School Bowling USA
615 Six Flags Dr.
Arlington, TX 76011
(800) 343-1329 / FAX: (817) 633-2940
kris@bpaa.com

International Bowling Museum & Hall of Fame
111 Stadium Plaza
St. Louis, MO 63102
(314) 231-6340 / FAX: (314) 231-4054
www.bowlingmuseum.com

International Bowling Pro Shop and Instructors
Association (IBPSIA)
4337 N. Golden State Blvd.
Suite 109
Fresno, CA 93722
(559) 275-9245 / FAX: (559) 275-9250
www.ibpsia.com

International Candlepin Bowling Association
3 Arrowhead Dr.
Bow, NH 03304
(603) 230-9665
www.bowlcandlepin.com

Multi-Unit Bowling Information Group (MUBIG)
1600 Pennsylvania
York, PA 17404
(717) 845-1504 / FAX: (717) 854-6072

National Bowling Association (TNBA)
377 Park Ave. S. 7th Floor
New York, NY 10016
(212) 689-8308 / FAX: (212) 725-5063
www.tnbainc.org

National Deaf Bowling Association (NDBA)
950 Highway 1 North
McGehee, AR 71654-9705
TDD: (870) 222-5640 / FAX: (870) 222-5641

National Duckpin Bowling Congress
4991 Fairview Ave.
Linthicum, MD 21090
(410) 636-2695 / FAX: (410) 636-3256
www.ndbc.org

National 500 Bowling Club
2116 Brown St.
Davenport, IA 52804
(319) 326-2645

National 600 Bowling Club
305 Penfield Place
Dunellen, NJ 08812
(732) 752-7049
www.natl600.freeservers.com

North Pointe Insurance Company
(Specialists in Bowling Center Insurance)
28819 Franklin Rd.
Southfield, MI 48034
(800) 229-6742
www.npic.com

Professional Bowlers Association (PBA)
719 Second Ave.
Suite 701
Seattle, WA 98104
(206) 332-9722
www.pba.com

Professional Women's Bowling Association (PWBA)
7171 Cherryvale Blvd.
Rockford, IL 61112
(815) 332-5756 / FAX: (815) 332-9636
www.pwba.com

Qubica
8800 Strike Lane
Bonita Springs, FL 34134
(800) 922-9559
www.Qubica.com

700 Bowling Clubs of America
1144 East Columbia
Davenport, IA 52803-1939
(319) 324- 7304
E-mail: Natl700@juno.com

USA Bowling
5301 S 76th St.
Greendale, WI 53129
(800) 514-BOWL
(414) 421-9008 / FAX: (414) 421-9188
www.bowl.com

Women's International Bowling Congress (WIBC)
5301 S 76th St.
Greendale, WI 53129-1191
(800) 514-BOWL
(414) 421-9000 / FAX: (414) 421-4420
www.bowl.com

Young American Bowling Alliance (YABA)
5301 S 76th St.
Greendale, WI 53129-1192
(800) 514-BOWL
(414) 421-4700 / FAX: (414) 421-1301
www.bowl.com

Index

About the Author

Don Williams is an executive for an insurance company that specializes in insuring bowling centers. Prior to that he was a bowling proprietor in Michigan for eighteen years. While a proprietor, he served on numerous local, state, and national bowling association committees and was elected President of the Bowling Centers Association of Southeastern Michigan and the Bowling Centers Association of Michigan. He has been awarded two meritorious service awards from the Greater Detroit Bowling Association as well as several citations and awards recognizing his charitable activities while a bowling proprietor. This is his second book about bowling.

**Use this convenient coupon for
ordering additional copies of
*The NEW Bowling Trivia Book!***

Name: _____

Address: _____

City: _____ State: _____ Zip Code: _____

Order	Quantity		_____
	Price		$9.95/book*
	Subtotal		_____
	Shipping & Handling		$3.00/book*
* Canadian residents, please pay $12.95/book and $4.00 for shipping.	Total		_____

Please send check or money order (no cash or CODs
accepted) to: Evergreen Publishing Group Inc.
28819 Franklin Road
Suite 710
Southfield, Michigan 48034

Order Online at www.bowlingtrivia.com

For information on quantity pricing, please write to the
address above or call 248-359-9990. Please allow 2-3
weeks for delivery.